HUGH LAURIE
THE BIOGRAPHY

HUGH LAURIE
THE BIOGRAPHY

ANTHONY BUNKO

JOHN BLAKE

Published by John Blake Publishing Ltd,
3 Bramber Court, 2 Bramber Road,
London W14 9PB, England

www.johnblakepublishing.co.uk

www.facebook.com/Johnblakepub facebook
twitter.com/johnblakepub twitter

First published in hardback in 2010
This edition published in 2011

ISBN: 978-1-84358-364-6

British Library Cataloguing-in-Publication Data:

A catalogue record for this book is available from the British Library.

Design by www.envydesign.co.uk

Printed in Great Britain by CPI Bookmarque, Croydon, CR0 4TD

1 3 5 7 9 10 8 6 4 2

Papers used by John Blake Publishing are natural, recyclable products made
from wood grown in sustainable forests. The manufacturing processes conform
to the environmental regulations of the country of origin.

Every attempt has been made to contact the relevant copyright-holders,
but some were unobtainable. We would be grateful if the appropriate
people could contact us.

To the Trinity Tiddlers, who leap-frogged
their way into our hearts.

CONTENTS

'THIS IS THE SORT OF STRONG AMERICAN ACTOR I'M LOOKING FOR!'

Hugh Laurie looked tired, more tired than usual as he shuffled in his seat. Outside, the sun had already descended, but it was still stifling hot as the late African evening closed in. The English actor had just returned to his hotel room after a full day's shooting of the remake of the 1965 movie *Flight of the Phoenix* and he was exhausted. He hadn't even had time for a change of clothing.

Along with the rest of the cast and crew, Hugh had been filming in the Namib Desert for nearly four months and it was starting to take its toll on all of them. It had been a tough shoot so far, especially for the crew because everything, including camera equipment and the giant set of lights, disappeared in the shifting sands most nights.

'Every camera setup was brutal for them in the heat,' Hugh later said. 'I'm still pulling sand out of my trouser cuffs and parts of my body that I will never get rid of. I still get a little nervous when I see an egg timer. But, to be honest, we were never further than one hour away from a cold beer.'

It was just before Christmas, 2003. Hugh sat in his dusty, dirty clothes with his three-day-old stubble in the bathroom of the Swakopmund Hotel in Namibia in southwest Africa, possibly not the best place or the best look for what turned out to be the most important audition of the 37-year-old's life. Or maybe it was just what was required? Perhaps it was all part of the masterplan.

It was the time of the year known in the acting profession as the 'pilot season', when actors the world over receive scripts of possible new pilot shows from their agents. Hugh said, 'At that time quite a few actors on the film were being sent things and were making tapes and sending them in because they wanted to keep themselves in the swim. So it was almost a daily occurrence that someone would say, "Oh, I just got a script, what do you think of it?"'

Tonight it was Hugh's turn to face the hand-held camera.

To be truthful, the actor who had made his name playing half-witted, goofy middle-class English characters for most of his career had been so worried about finding scorpions in his shoes every morning that he'd almost forgotten about the pilot script he'd received.

Jacob Vargas, Hugh's co-star from the movie, held a small camera in his hand. Unfortunately the shaving mirror in the hotel bathroom was the best light they could find. They were in a poor part of the world and basic facilities like electricity weren't exactly plentiful.

Behind Jacob, out of shot, another actor from the *Phoenix*

film, Scott Michael Campbell, not only offered moral support but also volunteered to co-read with Laurie.

In his hands Hugh held three pages of the script that had been faxed to him on the only fax machine in a hundred-mile radius. He wasn't quite sure about the storyline or the role he was auditioning for in the pilot of yet another new American drama; a pilot show which hadn't even been named up to this point. 'At the time I was thinking, "It's a pilot, that's all. Maybe 10 or 12 days' work,"' he said. 'I didn't assume it would go any further than that. Most times they don't.'

Yet Laurie could tell from just a quick read of the dialogue that it was different; it was good material and the character sounded very interesting.

Although an 'interesting character', Hugh didn't think for one minute that the role he was auditioning for was actually going to be the central figure of the proposed show. It's tradition on American television that the central figure is usually the morally good person, which in Hollywood also often means being good-looking with a 44-inch chest and a chiselled jawline to die for.

'The scenes I got described House and Wilson and I actually read for both,' explained Hugh. 'But I thought that Wilson was the main character. He was the sort of clean-cut hero who would save lives and do battle with evil and fight crime generally, and I would be the sort of irritable but soft-hearted sidekick.'

He admitted that it wasn't until he got the entire script a while later that he realised House was the main character. 'It wasn't called *House*. It didn't have a title then. So that was the biggest surprise, to discover they were going to make the whole show about this character and they were going to call it *House*. And they were making a show about such an apparently unlikeable and complicated guy. Usually on American TV the hero is very handsome and very good and they're saints, they're saintly figures. And this was an unusual thing, to have such a horrible man in the middle of the show. But I loved him right from the start, I just loved the character. He made me laugh and I just fell for him. I just liked him right at the beginning.'

Nevertheless, hero or not, main character or just a walk-on part, like most things Hugh has done during his career, he was determined to give it his best shot. 'I didn't want to fail again at an audition I knew I could have done well. Like every other actor I've done hundreds of auditions but nothing ever happens. So this time I decided that I was not going to leave the room smacking my forehead and going, "Dammit, if only I'd done this." I was sick of my own feebleness in the face of stress. So I worked hard at it and I did get it right.' He even improvised, using an old battered umbrella to lean on instead of a cane.

It wasn't the dialogue that worried him. 'It was like a piece of music. I felt like I knew how it should sound. It didn't have anything to do with medical accuracy or behavioural accuracy. These pages to me seemed like pieces of music and I just knew how they should be played,' he revealed.

What did play on his mind was the fact that he was required to play the role with an American accent. Although he had some experience from past performances to draw on, such as his role in the *Stuart Little* films, and of course various comedy sketches, he didn't want it to sound too fake.

'I could hear the character in my head,' said Hugh. 'The

rhythm of his speech. What he was hiding behind the meanness and sarcasm. I could see him very clearly in my head from the start.'

Hugh took a deep breath and talked at the camera. 'I apologise for my appearance but...' – he paused – '...things haven't been going too well lately.' A longer pause followed. He glanced at the floor for a few seconds and then, as if by magic, he seemed to transform into a different person – or maybe he was just being himself. It all seemed so natural. Gone were the comical facial expressions that fans of shows like *Blackadder* were used to. This was serious stuff. For the next few minutes it actually looked like he wasn't acting at all. In fact it was so convincing and effortless, he appeared to be just having an everyday conversation with someone else in the room, albeit in a fake New Jersey accent.

The drawl was just perfect – Laurie later credited this to '...a misspent youth watching too much TV and too many movies.'

So, with the audition recorded and the actor pleased with what he had done, the tape was shipped off and Hugh went for a hot bath and a long cold beer, not necessarily in that order.

He knew the odds of getting the role were heavily stacked against him. Firstly, being in Namibia at the time of the casting sessions wouldn't help his cause. Secondly, he'd heard a rumour that the producers were adamant about casting a 'quintessentially American person' to play the role of House; executive producer Bryan Singer (director of *X-Men* and *Batman Returns*) in particular felt there was no way he was going to hire a non-American actor for the role.

And lastly, it seemed that Laurie's age might go against him, as the pilot script called for House to be 34; although director David Shore revealed much later that he never wanted House to be that young or too good looking. 'If Brad Pitt had played the part, you would have gone, "Oh, shut up!" Shore said.'

However, life in TV-land has a funny way of sorting itself out and, bizarrely enough, Hugh's fake American accent was so convincing that Bryan Singer (who, by the way, later compared Hugh's audition tape to an Osama Bin Laden video) was completely unaware that Hugh was actually English. In fact, he had been so impressed that he pointed Hugh's audition tape out to everyone as a first-rate example. 'Now this is the sort of strong American actor I'm looking for, someone who is able to grasp the character!' he enthused.

A month after sending the tape away and while finishing up the remake of the desert classic, Hugh's agent phoned him with some good news. 'A month later I'd forgotten about it and my agent said the producers wanted me to fly to Los Angeles to test for "that medical show", economy class by the way, which made me pretty sure I was an outsider. The producers thought I was American, or so they say. I don't think it ever occurred to anyone an Englishman could play House,' Hugh said.

Of course the character he auditioned for is the now famous role of Gregory House, a complicated and irascible medical genius who heads a team of diagnosticians at the fictional Princeton-Plainsboro Teaching Hospital. In a strangely comforting way, the House character wasn't dissimilar to Laurie himself, an actor who, although very successful in his trade, has struggled with bouts of depression and self-doubt for most of his life.

In January 2004, Laurie briefly got off a plane in London to see his wife and three children before flying off again to the 20th Century Fox studios in LA for his second interview. Locally, better-known actors such as Denis Leary, Rob Morrow and Patrick Dempsey were also being considered for the part, but creators Shore, Jacobs, and Attanasio were as impressed as Singer had been with the British actor and they decided to cast Laurie as House. The rest, as they say, is history.

'People say, "You've written books, you've been on TV and in films," but I've never really been able to see that as a big achievement, or get a sense of great joy out of it.'

Hugh Laurie

PART I

FROM CAMBRIDGE
TO WODEHOUSE
AND BEYOND

CHAPTER I

'COMFORT WAS THE WORK OF THE DEVIL'

Hugh's father, Dr William George Ranald Mundell Laurie, or 'Ran' Laurie as he was known in his early life, was definitely a hard act to follow. Born in Grantchester, Cambridgeshire, in 1915, Ran seemed destined for greatness. With oodles of drive, dedication and passion he began rowing as a hobby at Monkton Combe School and continued in the tough sport at Selwyn College, Cambridge, in 1933.

All his hard work paid off and his sporting career went from strength to strength. He went on to row in the famous Oxford v Cambridge Boat Race in 1934 and then again 1935 and 1936, winning all three. In the boat alongside him was Jack Wilson, who later became his rowing partner.

AP McEldowney, the chronicler of Selwyn College rowing and founder of the UL Boat Club commented on Ran Laurie: 'There arrived at Selwyn a freshman who was not only the most famous oarsman Selwyn ever had, but also one of the most famous Great Britain ever had – WGRM Laurie. And we can truly claim him as a Selwyn oarsman.'

After university, the athletic Laurie was selected to row in the 1936 Olympics – in front of Adolf Hitler in Berlin – as the Stroke (the rower who sits nearest the coxswain and sets the tempo for the other rowers) in Great Britain's eight. The team eventually finished in fourth place, just missing out on a medal. Together, Ran and Jack Wilson put their disappointment behind them and went on to row for the Leander Club, one of the oldest rowing clubs in the world, winning the Silver Goblets at Henley Royal Regatta in 1938.

Of course when the Second World War broke out, Ran's sporting career was interrupted. He was posted to the Sudan and spent the next ten years there, eventually becoming a district commissioner. It was in the Sudan that he also met and fell head over heels in love with Patricia Laidlaw. The couple got married in 1944.

After the war ended, Ran and Wilson returned briefly to Henley in 1948, once again winning the Silver Goblets at the Regatta. The 'Desert Rats', as the two became known because of their sojourn in the Sudan, followed the success up a month later by winning the gold medal in the coxless pairs event at the 1948 Olympics, which was staged on their familiar Henley course in London.

Hugh's father described the final as 'A thoroughly satisfactory race. It was the best row we ever had and we finished about a length ahead of the Swiss, with the Italians two or more behind them, and we had a bit in hand.' Four days after the race, his wife Pat gave birth to their second daughter.

According to the people who know about the sport of

rowing, Laurie and Wilson are still rated the best pair of their generation and it wasn't until 1988 that a young Steve Redgrave and Andy Holmes matched their achievement by winning the Olympic title in Seoul. Indeed, the boat Laurie and Wilson used is now on show at the River and Rowing Museum at Henley-on-Thames, hanging above the boat used by Redgrave and Pinsent when they won the 1996 Olympics.

Incredibly, Hugh was almost a teenager before he discovered that his father had actually won the gold medal for rowing in the coxless pairs at the London Olympics. 'I didn't even know about it until I was around 12. I remember I went fishing with my mother on a lake, or the loch, as they call it in Scotland. We got into this boat and my dad took the oars and I remember at this moment I rather anxiously said to Mother, "Does he know how to row?"'

A while later the inquisitive young boy was rummaging around in the attic of the family home when he came across an old cardboard box hidden in a dark corner. In it was an old sock with something heavy in it. Hugh pulled out the object which, unbelievably, turned out to be an Olympic gold medal wrapped up in old rags. 'But then I found this medal. Hey! What the hell is this? Very odd. Although it wasn't actually gold because this was the first post-war Olympics, and gold, like a lot of things, was in very short supply. It was gold leaf over tin.' He was shocked, but it was a pleasing discovery.

Hugh still can't believe how modest his father was about his achievements. 'There were no frames, no glass cases, in fact hardly any rowing memorabilia was on show in the house. It was astounding humility of a sort that people would barely comprehend nowadays. Humility was a cult in my family. I sometimes wish he would blow his own trumpet a bit more, but I agree with him that modesty is important. You need to be realistic about yourself, not to think that what you are and what you do matters more than it does. Conceit is definitely a bad thing.'

Nowadays, a framed photograph of Ran Laurie and Jack Wilson receiving their medals takes pride of place over Hugh's desk in the house he shares with his wife Jo and their children Charlie, Bill, and Rebecca.

Hugh said about the fantastic photograph of the two sportsmen receiving their medals on the pontoon at Henley, 'I imagine they were playing the national anthem, Jack is loose-limbed and grooving and looks like he should be mixing a martini, and my father is very rigid, standing to attention. I sometimes wished my father could take that pleasure in himself. These were two really remarkable men. Tough, modest, generous and I like to think without the slightest thought of personal gain throughout their entire lives. A vanished breed, I honestly believe.'

What he also found astonishing about his father's rowing success was how it didn't seem to change him at all. 'Years later, I remember him as a halfway mark umpire at Wallington Regatta, sitting under a square yard of canvas in blistering heat the entire day with his Thermos and cheese sandwich at his feet while glossier men gave prizes in the enclosure and rode in the launch. He'd got a lot from rowing and this was the giving back. Yet saying that makes him sound pious, as if sitting there all day was a self-consciously virtuous act, which isn't right at all. There was no sense of virtue about him. But by golly he was virtuous.'

Years later Hugh recalls going out with his old man on the river to pick up some rowing tips. 'I rowed with him. We'd sometimes go out on a boat together. He was ferociously strong, a very powerful force to behold.'

Years after winning his Olympic gold medal Ran, together with Patricia and their two daughters, returned to the UK where he set about getting a job to support his family. Hugh explained: 'So he came back at 40 with a science degree, thinking, "Well, what am I going to do now?" and with two kids, he enrolled in medical school with a bunch of 19-year-olds.' Hugh is amazed at how well his father adapted. 'It's unthinkable now, but there were so many instances after the war of people who beat Rommel in North Africa and then went back to sell insurance or completely retrain and have whole new lives.'

And retrain was exactly what Ran did. In 1954 Hugh's father qualified as a doctor, working for 30 years as a general practitioner in Blackbird Leys, the council estate built to house the workers at British Leyland's Cowley plant near Oxford.

Laurie remembers the odd occasion he went out with his father while he was doing his doctor's rounds. 'I went on house calls with him,' Hugh explained, with a wry smirk. 'Usually I would sit in the car while he was inside lancing a boil or whatever. I mostly remember being at home answering the phone for him. This was in the days before answering machines. Being my father's son, I sounded like him, and before I could say, "This isn't the doctor," they would jump in and say, "Doctor, thank God! It's all exploded. I can't stop it." And with no obvious juncture for me to step out of the way, I would, you know...let's just say I'd reassure them. You're an adolescent. You're craving attention. "Well, it sounds like you're doing the right thing there," I'd say. Or, "Oh yes, it will probably be all right. Call back if the swelling worsens." As far as I remember, I never lost any patients.'

Nowadays, Hugh feels guilty that he is paid more for one episode playing a fake doctor than most real doctors earn in several years. 'It's a peculiar aspect of what I do. I often think about my father who was a physician and how strange it is that I am better rewarded for faking this job than he ever was for doing the real thing. Go figure. It doesn't seem right. He certainly treated more patients in an average week than I do.'

He added, 'My dad was such a good doctor and believed passionately in the Hippocratic Oath. He was a very gentle soul. If every son in some way is trying to live up to his father it is irksome. But here I am prancing around with three days of stubble because the part calls for it and faking being a doctor when my father was the real thing and a very good one at that.'

Even with his busy medical practice and family life, Ran remained active in the rowing establishment. He was a steward at Henley, a selector for the ARA (Amateur Rowing Association, now British Rowing) and became president of the Leander Club, among many other things. In his spare time he chaired the Oxford Committee of The Duke of Edinburgh's Award between 1959 and 1969 and the Oxford branch of Save the Children from 1986 to 1989. He was so well thought of in the local community that in 2005, it was proposed that a newly refurbished health centre in Blackbird Leys be named after him. Sadly it wasn't to be, and instead it was named The Leys when it opened a year later.

Hugh's mother, Patricia, was a housewife and on occasions wrote essays about her life as the wife of a district commissioner in the Sudan. Some of the short stories were published by *The Times*.

'I must say,' Hugh said proudly, 'I was surprised by how good the stories were. You spend so long thinking of your mother as the provider of socks and toast and Marmite. I suppose all children grow up with that egocentricity. But that makes it hard to imagine her having a life of her own. To think she could have got on perfectly well had you never existed.'

The couple had two daughters and one son before James Hugh Calum Laurie came along on 11 June in Oxford, England in 1959.

Although Hugh's first name is James, he has never used it. His third name, Calum, is the short form of Mael Calum, which translates from Gaidhlig (Scottish Gaelic) and in English means Malcolm. His brother's full name is Charles Alexander Lyon Mundell Laurie, and Charles now works as a lawyer and shepherd in Scotland.

Alongside his older brother and sisters, Hugh grew up in Oxford, known as the 'city of dreaming spires', with an estimated population of just under 165,000. It is a picturesque city, famous for having the oldest university in the English-speaking world.

From an early age Hugh always looked up to his siblings, mainly because they were so much older than him. He was six years younger than his brother. 'They seem to be rather more grounded, well, wiser,' Hugh has commented. 'To me, they had all the answers. I felt I was the only one who had problems. Their version of things is that it was all ice cream for me,' he said. 'I don't know which of us is right. I don't remember being hideously indulged, but my siblings might tell you a different story. I was sort of an only child, because I was so much the youngest, sort of alone.'

Being 'alone', as he describes it, led Hugh to develop a vivid fantasy life, which he says made it extremely easy to imagine himself in other lives. It's something which still accompanies him today and he says he doesn't know what he would do without it.

With both his parents being of Scottish descent and members of their local Presbyterian church, it was only natural that Hugh would be raised the same way. The Scottish Presbyterian religion is known for having an ethic of strictness and self-denial and in Hugh's household, run-of-the-mill things like television and films were a rare treat. And Presbyterian values have stayed with him. 'I had a wonderful if uneventful upbringing,' said Hugh. 'My parents were very loving, but there's no question they were suspicious of ease and comfort. My mother was the first person I can think of who was into the idea of recycling. In about 1970, she was collecting newspapers from the whole village, baling them up and taking them to a paper mill. She'd get a shilling a half ton or something.'

One newspaper reporter once asked a glum-looking Laurie why he rarely looked happy and as quick as a flash he replied, 'Scottish Presbyterians are not supposed to look happy.'

Even today his strict upbringing clashes strongly with his current 'Hollywood' lifestyle. To try to compensate, he often denies himself the small pleasures of life. For example, when he bought a new car, he chose the only one in the showroom without central locking and electronic windows. 'It's odd, but

I chose the only one with manual everything,' he recalls. 'In fact, I think it's called the Volkswagen Presbyterian. It drives my wife mad having to lean over to lock every door and close every window.'

Hugh has since become an atheist, and being truthful as always, has said the religious aspect of his life has never meant much to him. 'I admire the music, buildings and ethics of religion but I come unstuck on the God thing. I don't believe in God, but I have this idea that if there were a God, or destiny of some kind looking down on us, that if he saw you taking anything for granted he'd take it away.'

One thing he did inherit from his Scottish roots was the wearing of kilts, which he still does with pride when the right occasion comes along. Quite unusual for a boy who was born and raised in the south of England.

Hugh's upbringing may have been strict at times, but he sometimes wishes he had a tougher upbringing – perhaps one similar to the teenage life experienced by his writing partner Stephen Fry. But behind the façade of his 'cosy' existence, Hugh's life did have its problems, and one major issue was with his mother. 'And she with me,' he said. They had a somewhat strained relationship, and Hugh found it a constant battle to live up to her high expectations and to deal with the 'heavyweight unhappiness' which marked his teens.

'I was an awkward and frustrating child,' he says. 'She had very high expectations of me, which I constantly disappointed. She had moments of not liking me. When I say moments I use the word broadly to cover months. She was contemptuous of the goal of happiness, of contentment, ease, comfort. She disliked even the word comfort.'

There were moments of kindness and good humour between them and times where she was a joy to be with, but from what he remembers it didn't last long. Maybe it was because with his father's involvement in work and sport she took on the role of the main disciplinarian in the household. Hugh felt she struggled to show him any affection. 'She could switch off. She would spend days, weeks, even months, nursing some grievance. I don't know if she was clinically depressed, but she certainly had mood swings. She used to get very angry with me. Actually, I think she found me a disappointment in many ways. It was much harder to get a tick in the box from my mother and I often felt she didn't like me. She had hostility to softness. She'd say, "Don't be so wet." I suppose I'm making it sound as if we were whipped every morning and sent on 20-mile runs. It wasn't like that. But you renounced things that made life more agreeable.'

It is the memory of these dark periods with his mother, rather than the lighter times with his father, which he uses to help him get into role when playing House. 'My character doesn't believe in softening the blow for patients,' he says. 'Humility was considered a great virtue in my family household. No show of complacency or self-satisfaction was ever tolerated. Patting yourself on the back was definitely not encouraged, and pleasure or pride would be punishable by death.'

This lack of encouragement also meant family members were not very expressive towards each other. 'We didn't talk about each other much except in a flippant way. We didn't touch. I didn't kiss my mother as a child. It struck me in my mid-twenties that it's a standard thing to kiss your mother, and then we started doing it by agreement. Is that usual? I suspect it is.'

The strained relationship between Hugh and his mother led the way for Laurie to become even closer to his 'generous and enthusiastic' father, whom he idolised. In fact he spent most of his earlier years trying to emulate him and at one point he even considered following in his father's medical footsteps. 'My father had high hopes for me following him into medicine. I wanted to and I had an interview at the London Hospital in Whitechapel, which is where my father had studied, and in fact I came very close to going there. I forget now why I didn't do so, probably I was too stupid, or too lazy, to commit to the necessary eight years of study. I wanted to and was going to choose the right subjects at school, but in the end I copped out. Medicine is awfully hard work and you have to be rather clever to pass the exams.'

Not living up to the high standards set by his father, both professionally and in his career as a sportsman, is a source of great guilt for Hugh and it weighed heavily on his shoulders. 'There was pressure, but it was self-imposed,' he says. 'My father certainly never pushed me. I wanted to emulate him in all sorts of ways. Of course I failed him in all sorts of ways, athleticism being one of them.'

In the end, Hugh finally gave up trying to be 'another Ran Laurie' and moved on to live his own life and to achieve his own goals.

Hugh's mother, Patricia, died from motor neurone disease when Hugh was 29. According to Hugh, it took her two years to die and she suffered 'painful, plodding paralysis' while being cared for by Ran, whom he called 'the sweetest man in the whole world'.

Hugh never reached any kind of resolution with the woman

who expected so much of him and whom he felt he constantly disappointed. 'No, no resolution, not at all. Or maybe very, very slightly. A small amount of movement, maybe two inches along a road of half a mile.'

Hugh's father later remarried Mary Arbuthnott in 1990, in Norfolk. He died from Parkinson's disease in 1998 at the age of 83. Hugh is open about the fact that he wishes his dad could have seen what he's achieved. The actor thinks his old man would have been extremely proud but maybe appalled at his character in the hit American TV show. 'My father was a very polite man, a very gentle, soft-spoken fellow. He did not like arrogance and he would have been appalled by the way House occasionally conducts himself. Very English, my dad. Reserved in that way. My father was about as far from the character of House as is possible to imagine,' he says. 'He was far more like Dr Finlay, a solid citizen who wore tweed suits and was overflowing with good sense and kindness.' Hugh did add on a lighter note, 'My father would have enjoyed seeing all the medical equipment, if nothing else.'

Of course he misses both his mother and his father, although he's quick to point out it's not their company he grieves for. 'I was so separate from them for such a long time. I went to boarding school at an early age, and once you leave home like that, things are never the same again. No, what I miss is the knowledge that they are there. My father, a lovely man, died a few years ago when I was in the States. I knew he was unwell and before I went I made a deliberate decision not to resolve things, not to have that final conversation. I didn't say goodbye and have the big talk.' Because, he says, 'I didn't want to give him my permission to leave. I wanted him to have unfinished business, as if resolving things would somehow be unlucky. I guess I was scared to let him clear the in-tray. I regret that now, but probably I would do the same again.'

On reflection, he wondered if he should have handled the situation with his father differently. 'I would have found it very hard to have had that resolving conversation. I looked up to my father too much to really open my heart to him. We were almost formal. I did not tell him I loved him. All I can do is hope that he would have known. If I'd said, I love you. Probably he would have been startled that I'd felt it necessary to say something that was perfectly obvious. That is what I hope, anyway.'

When Hugh wrote his best-selling novel, *The Gun Seller*, he dedicated the book to his late, great father. 'I thought he'd be rather pleased by it. But suddenly it dawned on me that actually he was, if anything, slightly embarrassed by the fact that he had received a dedication in a book that contained profanity, not to mention sex and violence. He didn't quite know how to cope with that.'

'I wouldn't say my father was uptight, but upright and pathologically shy. I suppose I get a lot of my character from him, also my mother. Humility was the quality she admired above all. Comfort was the work of the devil. Dad wasn't joyless. He had a strapping Presbyterian heartiness. My mother took it even further. She was a complicated personality and we had our good times and bad.'
Hugh Laurie

CHAPTER 2

'LUGUBRIOUSLY
SEXY, LIKE A
WELL-HUNG EEL'

Despite being reasonably well off, Hugh's parents still made big financial sacrifices for him to attend a succession of private schools. As he is more than happy to point out, 'I went to a very posh school with some very posh people, but I'm not especially posh myself.'

While growing up, Hugh enjoyed a typical private school education. First he attended the prestigious Dragon School where, like lots of kids of primary school age, he dreamt of being an action man or a policeman, or at a push maybe an actor. The Dragon School, founded in 1877, is a British coeducational preparatory school in the city of Oxford. Primarily a boys' boarding school, it also takes day pupils and in 1994 opened its doors to girls for the first time. Emma Watson, who starred as Hermione Granger in the series of *Harry Potter* films, and British tennis player Tim Henman, also attended Dragon Prep.

Like many other prep schools, the Dragon has a number of long-standing traditions, the more notable among them being the custom of calling the teachers by their nicknames – Inky, Guv, Smudge, Moocow, Lofty, Jumbo, Splash and many others – to their faces. Female teachers were called Ma – Ma Jones for example. To the army of *Blackadder* fans, the teachers' nicknames would sound incredibly like the famous scene from *Blackadder Goes Forth*, where Hugh explains to Captain Blackadder what happened to all of his old 'Trinity Tiddlers' school chums (Jacko, Badger, Drippy, Bumfluff) as they merrily leapfrogged their way down to the Cambridge recruiting office, and then played tiddlywinks in the queue before they signed up to fight in the war.

After Dragon School, like his father, Laurie attended one of the most famous British public schools, Eton College, often referred to simply as Eton. Britain's best-known independent boarding school for boys, it was founded in 1440 near the impressive Windsor Castle by King Henry VI as 'The King's College of Our Lady of Eton beside Windsor'.

It is one of the original nine English public schools in the UK and, traditionally referred to as 'the chief nurse of England's statesmen', it has been described as the most famous public school in the world.

Early in the 20th century, a historian of Eton wrote: 'No other school can claim to have sent forth such a cohort of distinguished figures to make their mark on the world'. And that person wasn't far wrong, as Eton has produced a very long list of distinguished former pupils, including 19 British Prime Ministers. Hugh had a fairly happy time at Eton and quickly settled into the workings of educational institutions without his parents. Like most teenagers, he did go through a somewhat crazy and rebellious period: when he was about 16 he innocently believed the world was against him and that minority terrorist groups like the Baader-Meinhof Gang and the Red Brigades were to be supported and encouraged. Today, the memory of this naive misjudgement causes him so much embarrassment that he can 'hardly speak' about it without blushing.

It was also around that age that he and the same band of friends took a pledge that they wouldn't live beyond 40. 'We decided we'd kill ourselves. In fact, there were some hardcore members of the group, I wasn't one of them, who wanted to make it 30. "I hope I die before I get old" sort of thing. Talk about arrogance. The arrogance of youth, it trumps all. We felt we knew absolutely everything there was to be known and the future held only decay and compromise and defeat. We vowed to get out of here before that happened. It's an interesting problem, isn't it? Because it's hard to know whether your 15-year-old self is the true expression of who you are and everything that follows is a sort of diluted, watered-down, compromised version of that, of all those ideas and dreams you've had and that sort of fiery essence you had at 15. Or whether actually you're just a sort of pencil sketch at 15. Which is the true you?'

While at Eton, Hugh admits that he definitely lacked drive and ambition and rarely pushed himself academically. He regarded himself as quite lazy, but clever enough not to need to work too hard. He confessed to cheating on French tests, smoking in the school loos, and moving his lips when he read. His school reports were desperate. 'I was lazy. I lied, about everything, all the time. I was a fussy eater. Once Mum caught me with two pieces of liver in my pocket and sent me back to the table to eat it. It took three hours and then I caved in. I gave up on the piano. That was a battle I won. I went on a hunger strike and didn't eat for three days.'

But it wasn't all anarchy, suicide pacts and indolence; Hugh did actually progress to become house captain and excelled in certain, less academic, subjects. He proved to be an extremely gifted musician – and still is – and played percussion in the school orchestra. But it was rowing that captured Hugh's full attention, as it had captured his father's. The 6ft 2in Laurie became a 'wet bob' at Eton, a term given to a member of the school's prestigious rowing team.

In 1977, Hugh and his junior coxed partner, J.S. Palmer, won the British national title before representing Britain's youth team at the Junior World Rowing Championships in Finland, the international rowing regatta open to rowers aged 18 or younger. There, Hugh and Palmer came fourth. In 1980, they were runners-up at the annual Henley Royal Regatta in the Silver Goblets and Nicklass Challenge Cup in the coxless pairs race for Eton Vikings (rowing) Club; they became the only British crew to reach the final, just losing out to the favourites, the American crew.

'I raced at Henley in 1980 in the finals of the Silver Goblets,' recalls Hugh. 'It was a very bad year to pick. The regatta had been overrun by the American Olympic squad who were looking to kick some sand into English faces after their boycott of the Moscow Olympics. With my partner, James Palmer, I squared up to two brothers by the name of Borscheldt, who were 19 feet tall and made entirely from

Kevlar. Or maybe they were Kevlar and made from Borscheldt. Anyway, they were munching canapés on the flight back to Boston by the time we finished.'

Later in life Hugh commented that to a degree there were similarities between his beloved rowing and the way in which his and other people's lives progress. 'With rowing you're facing backward, moving away from the direction you're facing. When you look at other people's careers, it's very easy to see things as being constructed, planned, devised, how they clearly got from A to Z through a series of calculated decisions. In actual fact, I think we're all facing backward, stumbling from place to place, from one thing to the next and it only takes shape in retrospect. "Oh, yes, I got here because I made this decision and it led to this place and that decision and this career." Which is how I went from wearing dresses to talking to mice to solving medical mysteries,' he continues. 'At no point did I ever have a plan. I was simply facing backward, doing my best along the way.'

As the youngest child, and spending long periods of time away in boarding schools, Laurie quickly learned the value of rib tickling and showmanship. 'I was a bit of a class clown, though not frantically so,' he said. 'I did know by age nine or ten, after winning a prize at school for acting, that funny was something I could do reasonably well. And, of course, it was just a way to show off to girls and to be noticed by all. That's how these things start; you try to make a girl laugh and then 40 years later, you still wonder if you're any good or not.'

Hugh got his first taste of acting at Eton but his motives were primarily aimed at improving his position with the opposite sex. 'My first taste came when I was around 13.

That's when I realised I quite liked being onstage. I knew especially I liked making people laugh, and girls, most especially. I was scared to death of girls at that age, but onstage, as a king in a school play for example, I would actually be seen by them, which is to say I wouldn't be completely invisible, as was my normal condition.'

Mary Nicholson, his classmate as well as the daughter of Hugh's housemaster at Eton, remembered him as 'the funniest person that I have ever met and the strongest character'. And she also felt that he was 'probably going to be extremely famous.'

However, showing off for young girls while onstage was as far as Hugh got with the opposite sex at that age. Life in a single-sex boarding school, on top of being painfully shy, actually gave him a late start with the girls. As far as he could remember in his life, he never asked a girl to dance, he never asked a girl out and he never had a party. 'Girls were strange, exotic creatures to be tiptoed around. A lot of blokes who go through the public school system suffer from a boyish dread of females and spend their teenage years being shy and awkward. P.G. Wodehouse perpetuated the idea that women are either so adorable that you are completely afraid of them and in their thrall, or dreadful old dragon battleaxe aunts.'

He recalls with dread playing a game with a gang of teenagers, where they had to tell each other who they would most like to kiss. 'There were terribly confident people who said, "Oh, I'd kiss so-and-so," while I was absolutely terrified and desperate not to kiss anyone because I knew I'd be so nervous I'd get it all wrong. If I'd been confronted with the necessity of kissing someone I'd probably have said, "Oh, my hamstring's gone. Can we wait until its better?"'

After several years of developing his sporting prowess at Eton, Hugh headed off in 1978 to study at Selwyn College, a constituent college of the University of Cambridge. It was the same college his father had attended years earlier.

The college, originally opened in October 1882, was founded upon the basis of the Church of England, with its aim being to encourage simple living and develop the Christian character in the student. It has always been a hotbed for producing a rich mixture of successful and famous people in various fields, such as Clive Anderson (comedian and television show host), Malcolm Muggeridge (author and journalist), Sir Edwin Nixon (managing director of IBM UK), John Sentamu (Archbishop of York) and many more.

Although Hugh went to Selwyn to concentrate on rowing, he still had to go through the 'boring' and 'inconvenient' decision of deciding what to study while he was there. Strangely enough for someone who classed himself as somewhat of 'a twit' and other such choice names, Hugh picked anthropology and archaeology as his major. Archaeology is the science of human cultures and understanding humankind, while its almost identical twin sister, anthropology, is the comprehensive study of human beings and their interactions with each other and the environment.

He later revealed in a whispered tone, 'I went there to row. It's been ten years and I think the admissions tutor can take it now...that's what I went for. And anthropology was the most convenient subject to read while spending eight hours a day on the river.'

Not surprisingly, at Selwyn he had little problem in the

prestigious rowing team and flourished in the tough and disciplined environment until a bout of glandular fever in 1979 forced him to withdraw from the rowing competitions for a while. He returned to competitive rowing a year later, going on to achieve what he had set out to do in the first place. He became a member of the prestigious Hawks Club, which is a members-only social cub for sportsmen at the University of Cambridge. Later, he achieved his major goal and won a Cambridge 'Blue' for rowing against Oxford in the annual Oxford and Cambridge Boat Race in 1980.

Only sportsmen and women at the University of Cambridge may be awarded a Full Blue (or simply a Blue), Half Blue or Second Team Colours for competing at the highest level of university sport, which must include being in a varsity match or race against the University of Oxford. A Full Blue is the highest honour that may be bestowed on a Cambridge sportsman or woman, and is a much-coveted and prestigious prize. In general, the Full Blue standard is approximately that of being successful at a national level of student competition, and the Half Blue standard is that of being successful at county or regional level.

The first ever Oxford and Cambridge Boat Race took place in 1829 and has been held annually since 1856, with the exception of the two World Wars. An estimated quarter of a million people watch the race live from the banks of the river, while around seven to nine million people see it on TV in the UK, plus an overseas audience estimated by the Boat Race Company of around 120 million; it is the most viewed single-day sporting event in the world.

The year Hugh rowed in the Boat Race, 1980, Cambridge

came from behind in the closing stages of an exciting race but eventually lost in a thriller by five feet (1.5 metres). It was a painful loss, one that young Laurie never got over. Losing by such a small distance in rowing is like losing a Formula One race by two seconds, or losing the gold medal in the 100 metres Olympic final by one hundredth of a second.

'I was rowing in the number-four seat in this particular encounter,' Laurie says, 'and the result was a loss by Cambridge by a distance of five feet, which is something which I will carry to my grave. In fact, I really shouldn't say this, because I still to this day wouldn't want to give any pleasure or satisfaction to the opposing crew. But yes, it's true. It was a very bitter defeat.'

Other than 'that' loss to the enemy, Hugh's rowing experience at Cambridge could be viewed as a success by everyone, other than perhaps by Hugh himself. Yet it was what he actually did while regaining his health in that first year that changed his life forever.

'It happened by sheer fluke. I'd gone to Cambridge University to become an oarsman, but I met this woman called Alison in the student bar one night. I'd told a joke or something and she said, "You've got to come with me." She took me to this club and said, "Here are these people doing the Footlights. You've got to audition." So I did and off it went.'

Cambridge University Footlights Dramatic Club, commonly referred to simply as the Footlights, is an amateur theatrical club founded in 1883 and run by the students of Cambridge University and Anglia Ruskin University. The club's reputation grew enormously in the 1960s as it became known as a hotbed of comedy and satire, and it still continues today. At the end of each year a show called the *Cambridge Footlights Revue* is put on by up-and-coming comedians and in the past has helped launch the careers of some of the cream of the crop as far as British comedy is concerned. These include John Cleese, Graham Chapman and Eric Idle of *Monty Python* fame; the three members of *The Goodies* (Tim Brooke-Taylor, Graeme Garden and Bill Oddie); Peter Cook, Sacha Baron Cohen (of *Ali G*, *Borat* and *Bruno* fame); plus many famous writers including Alan Bennett and Douglas Adams who wrote the world famous *Hitchhiker's Guide to the Galaxy* and who much later wanted Laurie to star in the film version as the main character Dent.

Subsequently, with rowing put on the backburner for a year or so and his anthropology studies not going that well, Hugh joined the Cambridge Footlights and suddenly found himself heading off in a completely different direction from where he had ever dreamed.

Among his fellow Footlights troupe members at the time was the up-and-coming British actress, Emma Thompson. Emma was born into a family of famous performers and was destined to be a star. Her father, actor Eric Thompson is best known for writing and narrating *The Magic Roundabout* shown on BBC children's television in the 1960s and 1970s. Her mother is the Scottish actress Phyllida Law; Thompson's younger sister is actress Sophie Thompson.

The Oscar-winning star remembers their first meeting during their first term when both were auditioning for parts in the pantomime. 'I first saw him when we were auditioning for parts in the pantomime *Aladdin*. I saw him sitting there. He was gigantic, a fucking giant. He trained and ate all the time. He looked a bit like Indiana Jones, wearing a lot of khaki. I saw him sitting there and I jabbed my friend in the ribs and said, "Star. Star. Star!" I knew at once. He sat on the stage and did an impression of the Emperor of China trying to attract someone's attention. It was extremely funny and clever. He was always so funny, the funniest person I've met. I remember once driving back from some Footlights performance and hearing on the radio that somebody had been kidnapped and driven off in a Ford van. We were in a Ford van, so Hugh did a lot of struggling and thrashing around on the front seat to see if we would be stopped. And I laughed so much I had to stop for a wee.'

During their time together, the pair had a brief fling and much later in life Emma described Hugh as not only 'very, very loveable', but famously she called him 'lugubriously sexy, like a well-hung eel.'

This was a description Hugh considered bizarrely amusing and he simply replied, 'It's quite a confounding image, isn't it? I mean, are eels even hung at all?'

Yet they had a great time together and even when the fling ended, they still remained close friends and colleagues. 'We couldn't even imagine a life in Hollywood back then. Hollywood was as distant and impossible as El Dorado. It was all about fun. Watching Emma was like watching the sun or wind or some other elemental force. Her talent even then was inescapable. I remember she once did a monologue as a sort of gushy actress winning an award. I still remember the first line, "This award doesn't really belong to me." We thought, "This woman is so gifted, she will win an award like that one day, maybe even an Oscar." That was also around the time I met Stephen Fry.'

The meeting of Hugh Laurie and Stephen Fry will go down in comic folk law, like many of the great double acts down the years. Laurie was looking for someone to help him write and perform in Cambridge's big end-of-the-year production, the *Cambridge Footlights Revue*. Hugh was anxious to meet up with Fry after seeing a play Fry had written and performed, called *Latin*, in 1980.

'I first saw him on stage when he was 19. He had the right look, dark and melancholic. Stephen played an old man, but he was actually like that off stage. Even as an undergraduate of 20, he looked like he was about 55. He looked as if he'd seen a lot of the world. He's the only person I know who has got younger with time. He'll be in short trousers in about ten years. He was also about a foot taller than anyone else and had a very deep voice. I thought he would be an asset.'

The pair came face to face a few days later. 'So I hauled him in,' said Hugh, 'I basically gave him his first job and I constantly remind him of it.'

Fry remembers it well. 'Yes, well Emma introduced us. She said, "You've got to go and meet this old Etonian chap Hugh". So she took me to his room at Selwyn and he was there with a guitar in his hand. He said, "I'm writing this song, but I'm a bit stuck." We did some lyrics together, finished the song and then right away he said, "Now let's write a sketch." And this was before I'd had a cup of tea or anything! That was our first meeting,' he continues, 'and from then I was absorbed into the Footlights.'

Emma could tell straight away there was something special

between the two men. 'The instant they met, and they recognised something in each other. Laurie for a start must have been surprised to find someone taller than him; Fry is six foot four.'

To Fry, who had been through a stressful few years, meeting Laurie was the best thing that could have happened to him at the time, both in terms of his career and in terms of his emotional state of mind. 'He is absolutely my best friend. People sometimes call me a Renaissance man, but I'm not and Hugh is. He's a natural athlete. He's a gifted musician. He is clever, perceptive, has natural charisma. Sometimes it is thought that I'm the loud mouth and the dominant one, but we have been an equal partnership. And we have not been jealous of each other. I'm genuinely thrilled when good things happen for him.'

And even though they were having fun writing and performing together, neither of them really thought a career in the arts would beckon. 'For Hugh and I, it never occurred to us that we could have a profession in this business we call "show". I was content to stay here, growing tweed in the corner of some college with hair growing out of my nostrils by the age of 30. Hugh had a stranger ambition. He wanted to join the Hong Kong police force. He liked the ironed white shorts and he'd read somewhere, this is very Hugh, that they were corrupt and it needed good, clean Englishmen, or Scotsmen in his case, to go and sort it out. He fancied himself going in and being the incorruptible shining light of the Hong Kong police force, a sort of *Serpico* figure in splendid shorts. I think he rather liked that idea, half seriously.'

Hugh concurred with his partner concerning his ambition to

go into the Hong Kong police. 'We're all susceptible to images. For me it was probably *The Third Man*. I saw myself as Trevor Howard getting out of a Land Rover, being laconic and sucking on a pipe.'

Luckily for the world, neither of the Cambridge students pursued their earlier dreams and instead they continued to enjoy each others company and write the odd funny thing or three.

Between all the rowing and the acting, Hugh's studies came way down on his list of priorities. In fact, he finished college with a third-class honours in anthropology and archaeology to his name, which is the lowest honours classification in most modern universities. Roughly eight per cent of students graduating with an honours degree receive third-class honours.

But Hugh accepted it with a shrug of his broad shoulders. Even to this day he is apparently still more riled about losing the 1980 Boat Race to Oxford by a measly five feet than by achieving average grades.

Yet to the people who knew him, he was very clever. Emma Thompson knew Hugh wasn't a true scholar in the academic sense at school, but she loved the way he was such a lateral thinker and was so clever in many other things. Yet out of Laurie and Fry, she thinks Stephen is the cleverest and has a memory which is absolutely prodigious. He never forgets anything.

In that last year at Cambridge (1980–81), Hugh was elected president of the Footlights Club with fellow Footlighter and then ex-girlfriend Emma acting as vice-president. Traditionally, at the end of the year, the Footlights take their act on the road, starting in Cambridge, with a small tour of the country before ending up at the Edinburgh Festival. That year they took their revue *The Cellar Tapes*, written principally by Laurie and Fry, which included Thompson, Tony Slattery, Paul Shearer and Penny Dwyer, to the land of Hugh's ancestors.

The Edinburgh Festival Fringe, called The Fringe for short, was established in 1947 and is now classed as the world's largest arts festival. It takes place in the Scottish capital during three weeks every August alongside several other arts and cultural festivals, collectively known as the Edinburgh Festival, of which the Fringe is by far the largest and most supported.

The Fringe involves various forms of performing arts, particularly theatre, dance and music, but it's the comedy section which has grown in size and popularity over the years. The Fringe often showcases experimental works and as well as formal events, there are plenty of street fair shows taking place. In 1981 the first ever Perrier Awards for Comedy was introduced, and in its first year the prestigious award went to Hugh and the others for *The Cellar Tapes*. It was to open up many new and interesting opportunities for the troupe of actors from Cambridge.

The Times described the show as follows: 'The Cambridge revue, *The Cellar Tapes*, is just about the most entertaining, the most delightful, the most thoroughly good-time show that I have seen for years...their satire has enormously improved.'

Laurie commented on the success of the show that he helped mastermind. 'We took it to the Edinburgh Festival and won an award. We didn't know what that was, so it was a bit of a fluke. Part of the prize was a week long run at a theatre in London where we got good reviews. As a result,' he added dryly, 'neither of us had to work down a coal mine for ten years before getting our big break. I'm afraid there have been no real jobs.'

One of the rewards for winning the 'Pick of the Fringe' award was a three-month stint in Australia. It was a tour of which Emma said that by the time they all came back, Fry and Laurie were so close and on the same wavelength that they were almost married.

A modified version of the show, titled *Beyond the Footlights*, returned to London in the spring of 1982, and a television version was also broadcast in May of that year. Their success with the revue led to many doors opening for Fry, Laurie and Thompson, doors which would probably have never been accessible if they hadn't been lifted into the spotlight.

Hugh found it amusing, and thoroughly confusing, how he stumbled onto the road to his future in the arts more by accident than design. The whole idea of acting, especially messing around doing comedy with the hope of actually making a living out of it, seemed alien to the quiet and modest boy from Cambridge. Even today with all the success he has achieved worldwide, it still hasn't really sunk in. 'I've really drifted for so much of my life, I've made very, very few decisions,' the star said. 'I sort of just tumbled along and then, when I was in my last year at Cambridge, a man pulled up in a Bentley with a long cigar and said, "I'm an agent, do you want to do this acting thing for a living?" Which is, like, ridiculous really, that I wasn't tested. I've never had to pay any great price for what I do, and I sometimes feel a bit guilty about that.'

He still has trouble understanding how such an annoying kid who talked back and made a fool of himself in front of the school at times could become successful. 'Acting is not an English thing to do. It's not a thing that schoolteachers ever advise kids to look into or take seriously. In fact, generally speaking, they probably frown on it. "Sure, you want to play around with it, but grow up and get a proper job." Which is something I plan to do very soon.'

Fry is also grateful for the opportunity that came their way. "I think all of us who have had obvious advantages like private education and Cambridge and all that sort of thing are bound to feel, if not guilty, then at least we owe the world something. I think that's a natural and healthy thing.' And Fry believes his friend's ad-hoc start in the business has been liberating. 'I think one of the advantages of not being trained, of being educated, is that you are not an anything, you're not a noun. I'm not a comic actor, he's not a comic actor, we just do things, whatever comes up, whatever appeals.'

The Footlights troupe of '81 proved to be a very successful band of individuals who just happened to be in the right place at the right time and who blended together to form a very special team. In fact, most went on to even greater success. Stephen Fry, for one, went on to work closely with Laurie as an actor for a number of years as well as a writer, comedian, author, television presenter and film director in his own right. In addition to his work in television, Fry often writes columns and articles for newspapers and magazines, and on top of all that he has written four novels and an autobiography, *Moab*

Is My Washpot. He also appears frequently on BBC television and radio.

Emma Thompson went on to win two Academy Awards as an actress, comedian, and became a successful screenwriter. She was always the one who was going to reach the top first. Her acting talent was so impressive that while she was still at Cambridge, agent Richard Armitage signed her to a contract while she was still two years away from graduation. She never looked back and went on to star in the West End revival of the musical *Me and My Girl*, opposite Robert Lindsay (which was in fact adapted by Stephen Fry). That was followed by shows on TV like *Fortunes of War*, and the cult TV series *Tutti Frutti* for which she won a Bafta for Best Actress.

But it was in the world of movies that she really bloomed. Her first major film role was in Richard Curtis's 1989 romantic comedy *The Tall Guy* co-starring Jeff Goldblum. It was just the start as she reached unbelievable highs with a series of critically acclaimed performances beginning with 1992's *Howards End* for which she received an Oscar for best actress. She played a lawyer for the Guildford Four in *In the Name of the Father*; in *The Remains of the Day* she starred opposite Anthony Hopkins, and she was the British painter Dora Carrington in the film *Carrington*.

Thompson won her next Oscar in 1996 for best adapted screenplay for her adaptation of Jane Austen's *Sense and Sensibility*, a film directed by Ang Lee, in which she also starred. She has said that she keeps both of her award statues in her downstairs bathroom, citing embarrassment as the reason for not placing them in a more prominent place.

Most recently, Thompson appeared in supporting roles in

Harry Potter and the Prisoner of Azkaban and *Harry Potter and the Order of the Phoenix*. She has also appeared in the comedy *Love Actually*. She also enjoyed writing and adapting the film *Nanny McPhee*, from Christianna Brand's *Nurse Matilda* books.

Also from 1981's successful Footlights troupe, Anthony Declan James Slattery is an English actor and comedian who has regularly appeared on British television since *The Cellar Tapes* but most notably as a regular on the improvisation show *Whose Line Is It Anyway?* and the improvisational comedy series *S&M*, alongside Mike McShane. He has also appeared on other panel quizzes such as *Have I Got News For You*. As a dramatic actor Tony Slattery has appeared in *The Crying Game*, *To Die For*, *Peter's Friends* and *The Wedding Tackle*. He also appeared on the London stage in the musicals *Me and My Girl* and *Radio Times* and in the play *Neville's Island*. At the end of the 1980s, Slattery became a film critic, presenting his own show on British television *Saturday Night at the Movies*.

Paul Shearer is best known as one of the talented members of *The Fast Show* team, where he took on a variety of well-loved roles. He also appeared in adverts for the furniture store ScS as well as doing a large amount of voice-over work for adverts and TV shows.

Penelope Rosemary Dwyer worked as a writer and performer in Cambridge until her appearance at The Fringe, but unlike her fellow Perrier winners she chose not to pursue a full-time career in the entertainment business and instead turned her hand to becoming a metallurgist, which allowed her to play a major role in the construction of the Channel

Tunnel. Dwyer died in Somerset in 2003, aged 49, following a long illness.

'Hugh is a remarkable man, but he won't use his talents. He is a brilliant musician. He has a fantastic singing voice, which he'll never use, to my despair. And all because he's terrified of appearing cocky.'

Stephen Fry

'THE BBC HATED IT...'

Between 1983 and 1985, Hugh began to make a name for himself, although reasonably small, alongside his old chum and writing partner, Stephen Fry, in the world of show business.

In the early 1980s in the UK, comedy had turned into something of a safe and predictable wasteland awash with obviously talented yet comfortably wealthy and established comedians hogging prime time TV slots.

However, that was all about to change when a gang of fresh faced 'alternative' comics, or as many would say 'cocky upstarts', appeared out of the mist and on a mission to show the world there was more to life than mother-in-law gags and comic dance routines with newsreaders. Strangely enough, many of these upstarts would, later in life, go on to reach worldwide fame and fortune.

Very much like the punk rock revolution which happened in

the music scene years before and shook the music establishment to its very core, this gang of up-and-coming comics aimed to kick the comedy scene up the backside, or to be more accurate, boot it firmly in the nuts. And at that time, it was what the industry was screaming out for and importantly, what the youth of the country needed: a band of comics they could call their own.

The alternative gang consisted of two different, but extremely talented bands of individuals who surprisingly blended together quite successfully, even though there could well have been a clash as the two different cultures collided. In the red corner the real first wave of alternative punk-styled comics such as Rik Mayall, Adrian Edmondson and Alexei Sayle. These 100mph comics had burst onto the scene through less affluent universities or art colleges and worked non-stop in the comedy clubs of London. In the blue corner, from Cambridge, the more privileged members like Stephen Fry, Hugh Laurie and Emma Thompson were fresh from their exploits of the *Footlights Revue*. In between, maybe the most important figure of all to emerge, was the Don King of the alterative scene – none other than Ben Elton, a prolific writer with a motormouth and a brain to match, who floated effortlessly between both camps with outstanding ease and success.

However, as with all new wave movements, there's no use having ideas and attitude if there's nowhere to show it off. Luckily for them, Granada TV happened at that moment to be searching for a show to compete with the hugely successful BBC comedy, *Not the Nine O'Clock News*, which ran from 1979 to 1982 and starred Rowan Atkinson, Pamela Stephenson, Mel Smith and Griff Rhys Jones.

Sandy Ross, producer for Granada, approached the talented stand-up comic Rik Mayall in 1982 to write and star in a three-series show initially called *There's Nothing to Worry About!* Mayall agreed and persuaded the TV company to sign up Ben Elton as well as some other artists to work on the show. Granada agreed but then, out of the blue, Mayall left to pursue something else, leaving Granada with Elton, Fry, Laurie, Thompson, Redmond and Paul Shearer.

Laurie said, 'It's often assumed that anyone associated with Footlights is automatically favoured by television, but the producers saw a lot of revues before they chose us.' He added, 'We were incredibly lucky. *Not the Nine O' Clock News* had started and every other TV company wanted to do the same thing.'

Stephen Fry remembers the build-up to the show very well. 'Hugh and I were put together and told to write. We would normally write a quarter of a sketch to every 1,000 sketches Ben Elton would do.'

Laurie chipped in. 'Ben was just like a whirlwind...he would just blow us away. While we had one thing written on a back of an envelope, he'd turn up with so much material it was hard for him to carry it all. He would slap it down on the table. I can remember being absolutely amazed by his energy and by his certainty.'

Ben was also impressed with his new writing team but for different reasons. 'I'd never met people like Stephen and Hugh before. They seemed a lot older than me. Hugh's actually a pretty groovy guy, into motorbikes and blues, but at the time my impression was very much tweed and Cambridge. They both spoke very well. They knew about wines and they wore good leather shoes. I was quite enthralled. When we went up to Manchester, they put us up in the Midland Hotel. It was so exciting being paid to work on a comedy show, and to do it with these rather different people. The year before I'd been at Manchester University drama department, and there I was back in Manchester drinking wine and having roast beef with Stephen and Hugh and Emma.'

However all writers are different and that's not a bad thing. At first Fry and Laurie wrote quite slowly, in fact very slowly for young writers wanting to make a living in the fast-paced world of TV comedy sketches, especially compared to the machine known as Ben Elton. But what they did create were well-crafted sketches that were quite different in style to what was out there at that time.

When the pilot show of *There's Nothing to Worry About!* was aired, frustratingly only in the north of the country, it wasn't that well received by critics and audiences alike. But it wasn't considered bad enough by the powers that be to be axed so the TV company decided to give the team another go but insisted on some minor changes.

Out went actor Paul Shearer, to be replaced with the larger-than-life Scottish comedian Robbie Coltrane, who later found fame as criminal psychologist Cracker and starred as Rubeus Hagrid in the *Harry Potter* films. Even with Coltrane on board, it was still quite hard work because at the time, only Coltrane and Ben Elton had any real experience of working on this type of project in any kind of professional capacity.

The programme was also re-titled *Alfresco*, which came from the Italian *al fresco*, meaning 'in the fresh air', a reference to the decision to shoot much of the material outside the studio on location. Handheld video equipment was used, a bit like news crews used, instead of the more conventional and often more expensive way of filming. This innovation proved to be one of its strengths and *Alfresco* broadcast from May 1983 to June 1984, running for two series totalling 13 episodes.

'Absolutely no one saw it because it went out so late on a Saturday night,' said Laurie.

The show was comprised of a series of one-off sketches and several characters. Elton and Laurie appeared as Mr Butcher and Mr Baker, two odd gentlemen in a weird cinematic black-and-white setting using dialogue which relied heavily on wordplay. Alan and Bernard saw Fry and Laurie as two young men discussing topics such as war prevention, a trendy cinema and the SAS. The characters had appeared earlier in life in the *Cambridge Footlights Revue*. Another, Doctor De Quincy, saw Fry as the Doctor, a character that resurfaced in the sitcom *Happy Families* in 1985, which was also written by Ben Elton. The tone of the first series had a very odd and surreal feel to it. The cast were, as predicted, full to the brim with youthful energy and made a point of avoiding the stereotypical jokes about sex and racism which were around at that time. The humour that came across on the screen wasn't as twisted or as anarchical as some of the stars, especially Elton. In the second series in 1984, the overall style changed slightly. A linking device in the form of a 'pretend pub' was created, and the sketches themselves were less dark than in the first series.

While the series failed to have the impact Granada had hoped for, *Alfresco*'s ratings and feedback from the punters compared well with other contemporary sketch shows at that time.

'We learnt a huge amount about television through it,' said Fry. 'It came after *Not the Nine O' Clock News* and before *Saturday Live*, but I certainly wouldn't say we spoke for a generation. We were lucky. The gates were opened to us in 1980, and then shut very firmly a year later. There are still very few slots for young comedians and today's stand-up performer has nowhere to go unless he can act as well.'

Looking back now, the show may not have been the best thing on television, but it did serve its purpose. Firstly, it gave Hugh a chance to rub shoulders with some of the more alternative comedians at an early stage in his career, and helped him and Stephen to look at things differently from the 'comfortable' world in which they lived without losing their identity and style. Secondly, it proved to be the springboard the writing partnership needed to display their intellectual humour and special talents, especially when working together. It established Fry and Laurie's reputation as a comedy double act so much so that in 1983 the BBC offered them their own show, *The Crystal Cube*, a bit of a science programme done 'mockumentary' style, which spoofed some of the more serious science programmes at the time like *Tomorrow's World*.

This was a massive development for the young Fry and Laurie. The BBC had always been classed, and probably still is, in a different league when it comes to producing original comedy shows that stand the test of time. There are many, many examples over the years, such as *Fawlty Towers*, *Porridge*, *The Young Ones* and, of course, *Monty Python* to name just a few; whereas ITV was notorious for churning out average-to-bad shows which were more advert fillers than comic classics, and most of them better forgotten with the exception of a few odd gems among the dross, such as the excellent *Rising Damp* starring Leonard Rossiter.

Thus for the young writers to get a pilot for the Beeb, and to be able to also star in it, was like a dream come true. It was the first thing they had written together for TV from start to finish on their own so, not surprisingly, they wanted it to be perfect. Thinking of safety in numbers, they roped in some old friends such as Emma Thompson and Robbie Coltrane to play parts in the show.

Laurie was extremely excited about the project. 'We loved *The Crystal Cube*. We thought it was something no one else had done before and we thought there was a great comic possibility as we saw it.'

The concept was to discuss a different topic of science in each episode. The pilot show was hosted by a character called Jackie Meld, played by Emma Thompson, with genetics chosen as the topic for the show. Two guest scientists, Dr Adrian Cowlacey (Fry) and Max Belhaven (Laurie) of the Bastard Institute in California, discussed the issue of genetics to a live studio audience and viewers at home. The show also featured a lively debate between a member of the clergy, The Bishop of Horley, The Very Reverend Previous Lockhort, played by John Savident, and an anti-communist journalist called Martin Bealey, played by Robbie Coltrane, who went out of his way to claim the Soviets were going to invade Britain using genetics.

The show was broadcast on 7 July 1983 on BBC Two after 10pm.

'The BBC hated it,' said Laurie. 'Is that too big a word? No! I think hate was about right. They loathed it.'

He couldn't have been more right. Apparently certain people at the BBC did hate it with a passion. Maybe it was a case of poor communication because the Beeb didn't expect Fry and Laurie to make a show combining elements of science fiction and mockumentary; as a result, the show didn't make it past its first half-hour. The axing of their very first series was disappointing and it hurt them. It was a harsh lesson in the workings of the television business for the two Cambridge-educated writers.

Hugh said afterwards, 'Sometimes I feel I've chosen the wrong career. I don't have the mental equipment for it really. The sort of "to hell with it" attitude that actors and performers need. They need an element of, "I don't care what people think, what will be, will be."'

It was the first real blot on their landscape and the pair did not get a chance to make amends with another programme for the BBC until 1987 when they created the pilot for *A Bit of Fry and Laurie*. Nevertheless, they did make appearances in other BBC comedy shows around that time. One in particular, which was written by some old friends, actually became one of the biggest cult shows of its generation: *The Young Ones*.

The Young Ones was a popular British sitcom first broadcast in 1982 on BBC Two. It was originally the idea of Rik Mayall and his then girlfriend Lise Mayer, but the BBC suggested they add Ben Elton to the writing mix. This proved to be just the explosive ingredient the show needed and the anarchic, offbeat humour the three created helped bring alternative comedy to television in the 1980s and made household names of its writers and performers.

To the millions of viewers glued to the box, in particular youngsters around the country, it was just what they wanted and needed. It was a show they could call their own, with lots of humour and observations they could relate to. It became so popular that the show was voted number 31 in the BBC's Best Sitcom poll in 2004.

The two series of 12 episodes in total combined traditional sitcom style with violent slapstick, sub-plots with no apparent link to the main story and bags of surrealism. It revolved around four students living in a squat in north London, although many of the external scenes were filmed in Bristol. All four characters went to the fictional Scumbag College but were never seen attending the college and rarely, if ever, seen studying. Rumour has it that the show was influenced by the sitcom *The Monkees*, which also featured four characters and a landlord along with a musical segment.

Laurie appeared in only one of the episodes, 'Bambi', where the housemates appeared on TV quiz show *University Challenge*. There, the Young Ones pitted their considerably lower wit and intelligence against the posh kids from Footlights College, Oxbridge, which of course was a reference to the Footlights Drama Club at Cambridge University. The Footlights College team was excellently spoofed by Ben Elton, who appeared from time to time in the show alongside Emma Thompson, Hugh and Stephen Fry. It was a scene close to home for Fry, who had actually appeared on the real *University Challenge* while at Cambridge and had lost in the final to a college from Oxford. 'An utter disgrace,' he later commented.

The show itself must have rubbed off on Fry and Laurie in

the wrong way because during the eighties, when they shared a house together with a couple of friends in north London, it was said the place was such a shambles that it resembled the set of *The Young Ones*.

Because the show was such a big hit across the UK, even the actors who played relatively small parts throughout the series, such as Laurie, become known by the mass of fanatical viewers; the flood gates, which so far had been reasonably successful in holding back the alternative comedy tide, had now burst open.

After *The Young Ones*, Fry went solo for a short while and set himself up for a lifetime of financial security when he adapted the hugely successful 1930s film *Me and My Girl* for the West End stage in 1984, starring Emma Thompson.

Meanwhile, Hugh Laurie appeared briefly in a sort of spin-off sitcom of *The Young Ones*, again written by Elton with additional material by Rik Mayall, called *Filthy Rich & Catflaps*. Unfortunately, it didn't have the same impact as the madness and creativity of the original.

Next up for Laurie was a chance to dip his toe into the world of film with a small part in the movie *Plenty*. *Plenty* is a 1985 British drama directed by Fred Schepisi, adapted from David Hare's 1983 play of the same name. Laurie was very much a junior member among a cast of superstars including such names as Meryl Streep, Charles Dance, John Gielgud, Ian McKellen, Sam Neill, Sting and British comedian Tracey Ullman.

Set against the tumultuous events of the Suez Canal and Middle East crisis, in *Plenty* John Gielgud plays an ethical and scathing senior diplomat, while Meryl Streep is Susan

Traherne, a woman looking for solace and a decent life in the aftermath of the Second World War. Susan finds her life slowly disintegrating as she tries but fails to have a child before she marries diplomat Raymond Brock (Charles Dance) and suffers further emotional decline as her rather conventional marriage eventually falls apart.

Tracey Ullman and John Gielgud were nominated for Bafta awards, and Gielgud was also named as Best Supporting Actor by both the Los Angeles Film Critics Association and the National Society of Film Critics.

After that, Hugh settled back among old friends when he appeared in a sitcom called *Happy Families* with Fry and the rest of the alternative crowd; it was a rural comedy drama written by Ben Elton which appeared on the BBC in 1985 and told the story of the dysfunctional Fuddle family.

Happy Families also introduced a new batch of female comedy stars onto the screen such as Jennifer Saunders (*Absolutely Fabulous*) as Granny Fuddle, Dawn French (*The Vicar of Dibley*) as the cook, and Adrian Edmondson (Saunders' real-life husband) as her imbecilic grandson Guy. The storyline focused on Guy's attempts to find his four sisters, all played by Saunders, for a family reunion. The show also had a light sprinkling of more established stars throughout each episode including Jim Broadbent, Una Stubbs and Helen Lederer.

Ben, always one to experiment and challenge his writing, decided to film each story with a completely different approach. For example, one episode was shot to make it appear like a US soap opera, another like a French film, another, a gritty BBC documentary, and the last one like an

Ealing comedy. Unlike many other sitcoms, it was shot entirely on location and without a live audience.

Laurie was amazed at how prolific Ben Elton was even at early age. 'He's one of the cleverest people I know. It's fun just to be in his head. He's so very funny and very clever.'

At the age of 26, the sitcom made Elton the youngest lone BBC scriptwriter on a mainstream programme. Despite the fact that it was not a critical success, Elton still considers it to be one of the best things he has ever written. A budget was allocated for a second series but it was never commissioned and, as a result, the money put aside was used to produce the first series of *Red Dwarf*. Hugh Laurie actually auditioned for one of the main roles, Rimmer, in 1988. Unfortunately, he didn't get the part, which eventually went to Chris Barrie.

In 1986 and 1987, Fry and Laurie also wrote and performed sketches on the LWT/Channel 4 show *Saturday Live* in 1986. The concept of the show was a blatant rip-off of the long-running American series *Saturday Night Live*, except the British version tended to use stand-up comedy instead of sketches. A number of major comic talents appeared on a regular basis during the series' two-season run, notably Adrian Edmondson and Rik Mayall in their familiar guises as The Dangerous Brothers (Sir Adrian and Richard).

Presented by Channel Four and London Weekend Television from 1986 to 1987, *Saturday Live* weighed in with eleven 90-minute episodes, eight 75-minute instalments and two 80-minute specials. The show was briefly revived in 1996 and helped to introduce several new and important British comedy writers to the scene, including Charlie Higson and Paul Whitehouse, who as well as writing for various artists, also created and starred in one of Britain's best loved and popular shows in the 1990s, *The Fast Show*.

A second film for Laurie followed in between that time. *Strapless* was again written by one of the country's finest playwrights, David Hare, who used the movie to explore the eternal enigmas of love and desire. It is about two American sisters who try to come to terms with their womanhood in a Britain ruled by Prime Minister Margaret Thatcher. In the film, Hugh plays a young innocent doctor along side more established stars Blair Brown and Bridget Fonda.

It was another step up the ladder.

'You could say we're a manufactured friendship in that we were put together by a producer, but became real friends. Hugh and I and Stephen and Emma are the Spice Girls of comedy.'

Ben Elton

CHAPTER 4

'AS THICK AS A
WHALE OMELETTE'

One of Hugh's most memorable performances took place in the late 1980s with his wonderful appearance as two different characters, with all the same traits, in one of the most successful and best loved British comedy sitcoms ever. According to many TV polls, the *Blackadder* series rated alongside the likes of the outstanding *Fawlty Towers* and everyone's favourite *Only Fools and Horses* in terms of excellent storylines, razor-sharp dialogue and marvellous acting. As a matter of fact, in 2000, the fourth series, *Blackadder Goes Forth*, was ranked 16th in a list of the 100 Greatest British Television Programmes created by the British Film Institute. In 2004, *Blackadder* was voted the second best British sitcom of all time, topped only by *Only Fools and Horses*. It was also ranked as the 20th Best TV Show of All Time by *Empire* magazine and made household names of its stars.

For the millions that tuned in regularly, it must have seemed like comedy heaven as the writers of the show and the actors all suddenly peaked at exactly the same moment and in exactly the same place. It was a series that, like a fine wine, got better and better with age.

In total there were four series of *Blackadder*, plus several one-off shows, which meant it stretched from 1982 to 2000. Each series was set in a different era of British history with more or less the same core characters in each, supported brilliantly by a diverse cast of talent. Rowan Atkinson's Blackadder character was a cunning, scheming and often devious but loveable individual. Tony Robinson played his dogsbody, Baldrick, while Hugh Laurie, Stephen Fry and Tim McInnerny took on a variety of characters throughout the series alongside superb turns by Miranda Richardson as Queenie and Rik Mayall as Lord Flashheart.

The Black Adder was the first series of the *Blackadder* set, originally written by Richard Curtis and Rowan Atkinson, who like Fry and Laurie, had met at university. The two quickly became writing partners and, also like Fry and Laurie, had a massive hit performance at the Edinburgh Festival in 1979. As a result, they were given the opportunity to be the main writers (and in Atkinson's case, star in the show) for the BBC Two series *Not the Nine O'Clock News*.

Richard ,Whalley Anthony Curtis, CBE, a New Zealander by birth, went on to write some of the greatest and most iconic British films and TV sitcoms in British history such as *Four Weddings and a Funeral*, *Bridget Jones's Diary*, *Notting Hill*, *The Boat That Rocked* and *Love Actually*, as well as the hit sitcoms *Blackadder*, *Mr Bean* and *The Vicar of Dibley*. He won a Bafta, and was nominated for an Oscar.

Rowan Sebastian Atkinson, born in 1955, is one of the UK's

biggest comedians, actors and writers, famous for his work on sitcoms alongside *Blackadder* such as *The Thin Blue Line*, *Mr Bean* and voiceover work in Walt Disney's *The Lion King*. He has been listed in the *Observer* newspaper as one of the 50 funniest acts in British comedy, and among the top 50 comedy acts ever in a 2005 poll of fellow comedians.

Atkinson and Curtis came up with the concept for *Blackadder* while they were working on their hit show *Not the Nine O'Clock News*. They didn't want to compete with the wonderful *Fawlty Towers*, which was considered 'an impossible act to follow', so they decided to go back in time and take the mickey out of Britain during the middle ages with its issues including witchcraft, Royal succession, Britain's strained relationship with the rest of Europe, the Crusades to the Holy Lands and the conflict between the Crown and the Church. The first series also featured extracts of Shakespearean dialogue, which was altered slightly for comic effect; the credits at the end of the show featured the words 'additional dialogue by William Shakespeare'.

The choice of name for the show is believed to have Scottish origins but with strong links to British kings gone by. The first series took place in the Middle Ages in Britain around 1485, and apparently was written as a spoof history of the deeds of Richard IV and his unfavoured second son Edmund, the Duke of Edinburgh (who called himself 'The Black Adder'), Edmund's various attempts to improve his relationship with his father, and his eventual quest to overthrow him.

The first *Blackadder* series was initially aired on BBC Two from June 1983 to July 1983. It was a joint production between the BBC and the Australian Seven Network.

The first series had a sizeable budget for a sitcom of that time, which allowed most of the scenes to be shot outside on location. Despite this, it received mixed reviews with the critics and a lukewarm reception from the watching audience. Initially, the BBC decided not to continue with a second series, but luckily for Hugh, two strokes of luck came into play.

Firstly, in 1984, Michael Grade took over as the controller of BBC One and, after a frank talk with the team behind *Blackadder*, decided to give them another chance with a considerably reduced budget and with the proviso that the next script be funnier.

Secondly, and as important, Laurie's old friend Ben Elton stepped in to help co-write the show with Curtis, while Atkinson concentrated more on the acting side. It was then that the real magic of *Blackadder* began to take place.

'I suppose Richard Curtis knew I had written *The Young Ones* and quite liked it,' Elton replied when asked how he got involved in the first place. 'I said yes because I thought it would be great to write lines for Rowan.'

Besides adding more jokes, and some would say his left-wing point of view on certain matters, Elton suggested some changes of his own to spruce up the show. He was instrumental in many changes to the original characters' traits. Baldrick suddenly emerged as the stupid sidekick throughout the rest of the series, but a sidekick with his own famous catchphrases, such as 'I have a cunning plan' whenever Blackadder was in trouble. Meanwhile, Edmund Blackadder developed into a witty, clever and even handsome individual. It became a successful formula which continued throughout the entire series.

With Elton's edge and Curtis's strength with characters, the writing partners were a perfect match. Many agreed that Elton took a rough diamond and helped to mould it into a gem. The writing technique they devised was unusual in that they apparently never wrote anything in the same room together, but would instead each write three episodes separately and then swap them on computer disk for the other writer to change if he wanted. They had an agreement that if changes were made or parts were taken out, the original writer would just accept it. At times they both found the method to be a frustrating but fruitful way of being creative.

Ben's arrival on the second series also signalled the frequent recruitment of comic actors from the 'alternative' crowd for guest appearances, including Robbie Coltrane, Rik Mayall (who had actually appeared in the final episode of the first series as Mad Gerald), Adrian Edmondson, Nigel Planer and Jeremy Hardy. Elton himself popped up as an anarchist in *Blackadder the Third*. More establishment actors, some at the veteran stage of their careers, were also recruited for roles. These included Brian Blessed, Peter Cook, John Grillo, Tom Baker, Jim Broadbent, and Geoffrey Palmer who played Field Marshal Sir Douglas Haig in 'Goodbyeee...', the final, fatal episode of *Blackadder Goes Forth*.

Benjamin Charles 'Ben' Elton, born in 1959, emerged in the 1980s as a leading figure in the alternative comedy movement (the Johnny Rotten of the comedy world). He was already a successful stand-up comedian with a rapid-fire delivery style and sharp-as-a-razor observations. As well as writing other sitcoms like *The Young Ones* and *The Thin Blue Line*, he also starred in his own TV show *The Man From Auntie* and later went on to quickly establish himself as a successful novelist and screen writer turned film director with *Maybe Baby*, starring Hugh Laurie.

Not a writer to rest on his laurels and past successes, he changed direction in the 1990s when he partnered up with Andrew Lloyd Webber to create *The Beautiful Game*, which was nominated for 'Best Musical' at the Laurence Olivier theatre awards in 2000. His stage comedy, *Popcorn* performed at the Apollo Theatre, was awarded the 1998 Laurence Olivier Award for Best New Comedy of the 1997 season. He went on to co-write the Queen musical *We Will Rock You* with the band members themselves, and still not quite content with that, he did it all again with the works of Rod Stewart.

So with someone of Elton's obvious talent and drive on board, the new series of *Blackadder* suddenly took off and never came back down to earth.

Blackadder II is set in England during the reign of Queen Elizabeth I (1558–1603), who is played by Miranda Richardson. The principal character is Edmund, Lord Blackadder, the great-grandson of the original Black Adder. During the series, he often comes into contact with the Queen, the obsequious Lord Chamberlain Lord Melchett (Stephen Fry) and her demented former nanny Nursie (Patsy Byrne).

To make the show more cost-effective, it was shot with virtually no outdoor scenes (in contrast to the first series which was shot largely on location), and several indoor scenes, such as the Queen's throne room and Blackadder's front room, were used extensively.

It was during this second series in 1986 that Hugh made his first, but not last, appearance on the hit show playing one of

Blackadder's drinking buddies in one show entitled 'Beer' and as Prince Ludwig in another one called 'Chains'.

Blackadder the Third, set in the late 18th and early 19th centuries (a period known as the Regency) followed a year later. This was the series in which Laurie appeared for the entire term. With his over-exaggerated posh accent and boyish good looks, Laurie played the role of the inept idiot George IV, the Prince Regent, alongside a bitter and twisted Atkinson's down-on-his-luck butler Blackadder.

Hugh's performance playing the 'thick as a whale omelette' Prince George, who was more concerned with buying trousers and socks than dealing with matters of state, caught the public's attention and typecast him in the role of a bumbling half-witted fool for years to come.

Hugh commented: 'Ben and Richard had written some fabulous lines which gave me the opportunity to shout a lot and make faces, which is what I did well. It was enjoyable.'

Luckily for Hugh, the character of Prince George had only been added to the series as a replacement for Tim McInnerny's Lord Percy character, who did not appear in the third instalment because McInnerny ironically didn't want to be typecast.

The Prince George character was apparently modelled on George IV, although Laurie's physical appearance differed significantly from the actual appearance of the real George IV, who during his time of his Regency was grossly obese. Ben Elton and Richard Curtis, as usual, weren't in the slightest fazed by such trivial matters such as size and looks and throughout the show they went out of their way to ensure George was referred to as 'a fat, flatulent git'.

Fry remembers it well. 'Hugh's as thin as a rake but still stands in front of the mirror every morning shouting "fat git!" to the tune of The Great Escape.'

The final critically acclaimed fourth series of *Blackadder*, which many still say is the jewel in a well-decorated crown, was set in the trenches of the First World War on the Western Front in 1917. An unlikely setting for a comedy among the mud and stench of death, but writers Curtis and Elton both felt after reading up on the subject that it would be a perfect and a powerful environment for their situational comedy.

'Actually, all the lead up to the First World War was very funny, all the people coming from communities where they'd never bumped into posh people...and all being so gung-ho and optimistic...the first hundred pages of any book about the World War are hilarious, then of course everybody dies,' commented Elton.

Edmund Blackadder (Atkinson) is a captain who spends all of his time thinking of ways to escape from the idiocy of war and get as far away as possible from his stupid and repulsive 'trench buddies' and equally stupid senior commanders.

He is joined by old favourites, Private S. Baldrick (Tony Robinson), while Hugh pops up as idealistic Edwardian twit Lieutenant George. Stephen Fry plays the larger-than-life General Melchett who seems intent on ordering his men to certain death, and Tim McInnerny returns as Melchett's assistant, Captain Darling. Again there were some excellent guest appearances from Miranda Richardson as a field nurse and Rik Mayall back as the scene-stealing Commander Flashheart.

Hugh stepped easily from Prince George to Lieutenant the Honourable George Colthurst St Barleigh MC, a frontline officer who joined the army on the first day of the First World War along with nine other of his mates. The ten men named themselves the Trinity College Tiddlywinks, or the 'Trinity Tiddlers'. It is revealed later, in the fourth series finale, that George is the only surviving member of the group. To add to his persona, Laurie was supposed to wear a monocle as Lt. George, the character's second incarnation, but eventually decided against it after it kept falling out of his eye.

The extremely clever part of Hugh's character is the obvious progression he has made to the status of officer because of his background and special friendship with General Melchett (Fry) rather than his skills and competence in the role. Throughout the series he plays a loveable puppy-dog type character whose positive approach to life in the trenches really pisses Blackadder off.

Blackadder Goes Forth cemented the series' status as an all-time great, especially with its bold and highly poignant final scene from the episode 'Goodbyeee', when Blackadder, Baldrick, George and Darling charge over the top and into no man's land. The scene, which has no closing titles and prominently dissolves into an image of the same field filled with poppies, illustrates perfectly the darkest episode in the history of modern man.

That last scene alone exemplified the series' capacity to be more than just a sitcom, more than just a comedy show. It again showed *Blackadder* to be one of the most intelligent, as well as the funniest, British sitcoms of all time. It became a worldwide hit, winning four Baftas and an Emmy.

Laurie's performance, as both George characters, drew positive responses from critics with many shouting out that they considered him to be one of the best actors in the series, while others wrote that his performance as George was simply 'hilarious' and 'brilliant'.

'It was absolutely great doing it,' said Laurie. 'There was a real group feeling to it all, even though each of us had our moments.'

He did reveal, however, that the series still had its fraught moments behind the scenes, of actors and writers sitting in a room agonising over every detail about every word and every action. And there was a fair share of argument and disagreement about how things should go. 'It was quite competitive in a way,' remembers Hugh, 'but not unpleasant. It was kind of embracing. I remember whistling on the way to work. It was good to sit in a room and try to make each other laugh.'

Laurie reprised the role of Prince George in the Christmas special *Blackadder's Christmas Carol* in 1988, and also portrayed a new character, Lord Pigmot, set in the distant future. He also appeared in the millennium special *Blackadder: Back & Forth* in 1999, playing the Roman Consul Georgius and the modern day Lt. George Bufton-Tufton, The Viscount Bufton-Tufton.

Blackadder's Christmas Carol (mostly set during the reign of Queen Victoria, with some scenes taking place in the locations of the second and third series) was a 45-minute Christmas instalment. It was a twist on the Charles Dickens tale, *A Christmas Carol*, with Ebenezer Blackadder appearing at the start as a kind and loving man until the Spirit of Christmas Past turns up to show Blackadder the contrary antics of his ancestors and descendants. This snippet of information turns the nice Blackadder into the bad Blackadder that the audience loved.

Blackadder: Back & Forth was a 30-minute film originally shown in a special cinema at the Millennium Dome in Greenwich, London throughout 2000 and later transmitted by Sky and the BBC. It took a comical look at 2,000 years of British history, courtesy of a time machine that Baldrick constructs from da Vinci's blueprints. It provided the cast and writers that had grown-up with the series a last big reunion along with some other British stars like newcomer Kate Moss (as Maid Marian) and Colin Firth (as Shakespeare).

Hugh played Viscount George Bufton-Tufton and Stephen Fry played Bishop Flavius Melchett. A spokesperson for the production told the press: 'It is the best of British comedy to show to the world. Our sense of humour and our comedy is one of our greatest exports.'

In addition to these, two special programmes, *Blackadder: The Cavalier Years* (set in the reign of Charles I), were also made and shown as a 15-minute insert during the 1988 Comic Relief telethon.

Since the last tearful episode of the fourth series, when the cast climbed out of the trenches into the TV no-man's land, there have been many rumours about a possible fifth series on the cards, and there have been some wild and varied suggestions as to which time period it would be set. One of the strongest was a series set in the 1960s centred on a rock band called Black Adder Five, with Baldrick, aka 'Bald Rick', as the drummer and George playing the guitar and keyboard.

'Well, about 20 years ago we thought of doing a sixties one,' says Elton warming to his theme. 'That would be great! You could see a naturally conservative man like Blackadder up against all the excesses of the sixties, with Baldrick as a naturally bedraggled hippie.'

Another idea mentioned by Curtis involved Baldrick accidentally assassinating John F. Kennedy. And the possibility of a parody of Batman, called *Batadder,* was suggested by John Lloyd, the producer of the series. This idea eventually came to surface as part of the Comic Relief sketch *Spider-Plant Man* in 2005, with Atkinson as the title hero, Robinson as Robin, Jim Broadbent as Batman and Rachel Stevens as Mary Jane. Miranda Richardson and Tony Robinson expressed enthusiasm towards the idea of a series set in the Wild West, while producer John Lloyd favoured an idea for a series with a Neanderthal Blackadder.

Rowan Atkinson said he would very much like to do a new series set in Colditz or another prisoner-of-war camp during the Second World War, something that both he and Stephen Fry mentioned several times. Atkinson said, 'I like the idea of him being a prisoner of war in Colditz. That would have the right level of authority and hierarchy which is apparent in all the Blackadders.'

Atkinson also joked, 'There was a plan for a film set in the Russian revolution, a very interesting one called *The Red Adder*. He would have been a lieutenant in the Secret Police. Then the revolution happened and at the end he is in the same office doing the same job but just the colours on his uniform have changed. It was quite a sweet idea and we got quite a long way with it, but in the end it died a death.'

Ben Elton, in early 2007, stated that he hoped *Blackadder* would return in some form, whether it be a TV series or movie.

'The BBC would love it,' he said. 'It would be a bit of trophy broadcasting. But it was so long ago. Stephen Fry does look a bit fat and sweaty now and I haven't seen Tim McInnerny in many a long year.' However, he added, 'I don't think it matters a bit that we are all old. Everyone would love to do it again, but the burden of expectation would be too high.' He sighs happily. 'For a long time I kept thinking about a Victorian setting with Dawn French as Queen Victoria. Like Queen Victoria, she is very small and roundish. But unlike Queen Victoria, she is very amusing. And there is the idea of Neanderthal Blackadder. Then there was the Blackadder *Star Trek* notion, set in the future. I'm getting excited just talking about it.'

There was also talk of using Blackadder in lessons by some schools to teach the kids about history. Elton was amused at that. 'Clearly it is an absolute nonsense, but it has a certain historical integrity, and is done with a great love of British history. Blackadder does remind us that there is so much colour and splendour in our history, how filled with madness, love, hate and intrigue it is.'

Curtis jokingly remarked that Hugh Laurie's success on *House* may make shooting a new series difficult.

Realistically, it is too far down the line for Hugh to see it taking off now. 'I wish there was, but I don't think so unless Rowan loses all his money and is forced to do so. Also, the writers, Curtis and Elton, decided they'd had enough. I do miss it though,' Hugh said.

'Hugh wears his heart on his sleeve; he doesn't conceal anything. If he is nervous or depressed you can see it.'

John Lloyd, *Blackadder* producer

CHAPTER 5

'I THINK THEY WERE AHEAD OF THEIR TIME'

'We just made each other laugh all of the time,' Hugh commented on his writing partnership with Stephen Fry. 'Lots of the time we didn't make anyone else laugh but always amused ourselves.'

Laurie and Fry were acutely aware of each others strengths and weaknesses and the relationship between the pair had grown closer and closer since their first meeting at university. To the outside world they seemed to belong together like a pair of old comfortable slippers tucked neatly under the bed. And even though they are fundamentally very different people, they share the same sense of humour and the same way of looking at the world.

'When you are teenagers, friendship can be quite intense,' Hugh recalls of those early days. 'If you make each other laugh then you probably will for the rest of your life, and we still do. We can watch TV or read the newspaper and we find the same things funny at the same moment.'

As far as he can remember, Stephen and Hugh have never had a serious disagreement about anything they have done together. 'Doing what we do, which is vaguely creative, it has to be so personal and I couldn't imagine doing it with someone I didn't like or wasn't friends with. It would be so inhibiting. There's a lot of trust involved. The key to relaxation. You have to feel completely at ease. I don't think we've ever had a serious disagreement about the things that we do together. We sulk a bit, very rarely, but we never argue. Partly that's because we're scared of arguments. We each spend so much time running ourselves down that it would be pointless having the other person do it too.'

Stephen Fry is more than happy to agree. 'I think me and Hugh clicked from the first moment we met. Call it chemistry or alchemy, but we simply thought the same way. We have the odd sulk from time to time, but that's usually just sulking around with the world as much as anything. As for actual straightforward rows, we've never had them. I think it would be catastrophic if we did.'

Their bond remains strong even to this day, professionally and personally. 'I don't think I would have gone through this career without him,' Hugh says. 'I'll take the bull by the horns and say I love him.'

Whatever one does, the other one quickly follows, be it starring in feature films, writing books or attempting stage plays. 'Stephen was one of the first people I knew to buy a computer. I couldn't even use a typewriter. I preferred to write in pencil. He loves gadgets and all high-tech stuff. Gradually I was converted and I follow him in that. But when I started riding a motorbike again, and absolutely fell in love with bikes, he did the same and got a bike, leather jackets and helmets.'

As close as the duo is, the difference between them is also quite obvious, especially in TV interviews. Stephen is the one who usually dominates the conversations, the one who does 80 per cent of the talking. He uses the English language with such ease and control, often confusing even the most educated TV interviewer by throwing out the most unpronounceable words. Hugh, on the other hand, is usually slumped on the settee next to him, just content to throw in an odd funny sentence or a serious point now and again. Both seem very content with the roles they have informally selected for themselves, Fry always looking for attention, something that Hugh never craved at all himself. In fact, before Stephen arrived at Cambridge, he'd tried to commit suicide by swallowing enough pills to fill a bathroom cabinet and he'd been expelled from numerous schools. Shockingly, at 17 he was sent to prison for three months for stealing a credit card from a family friend; he was arrested in Swindon and as a result spent time in Pucklechurch (now Ashfield) Prison for fraud. It was a period in his life that Fry is ashamed of, although Laurie once said that 'He probably did it so he sounded interesting while getting interviewed.'

'The biggest difference between us,' said Laurie, 'is that Stephen can duel and I can't. I dread any competitiveness. I find it completely inhibiting. Stephen's fine with that. He can perform under pressure.'

'I think I'm rather more of a lion, circa 20 or 30 AD,' mentioned Fry. 'When Christians were in plentiful supply. I've always thought of Hugh as a panda, probably because he's not naturally aggressive. Either a Panda or an Opel Kadett.'

Yet Fry was quick to add, 'Hugh is one of the most intelligent people I have ever met. He really is, but he doesn't have the kind of awful chutzpah and smarminess that I do that sort of sometimes gets me invited onto *Question Time*. He's far too charming and nice.'

It wasn't always like that though. Thompson and Fry tell a story of an incident at Emmanuel College May Ball where they were 'the entertainment'. While on stage they were heckled and hissed at by the rowdy crowd. It got quite intense and quite scary. Some time later Fry recalled how the marquee began to shake. 'Hugh had some bijou revolutionary by the throat and was shaking him hard.' As the marquee collapsed, Laurie was heard in full tirade, 'Don't you dare insult my friends!'

With their friendship never in question and their nose to the grindstone, out of the blue they were granted a second chance by the BBC. After the failure of *The Crystal Cube*, Fry and Laurie were commissioned to write a sketch show, which aired at Christmas 1986: *A Bit of Fry and Laurie*. The pilot proved to be so successful that the programme was commissioned for a full series that ended up spanning four series and 26 episodes between 1986 and 1995. It helped cast the names Fry and Laurie firmly in stone in the British comedy hall of fame.

Laurie shrugged his shoulders as if he was embarrassed by his success. 'We did a pilot. They [the BBC] seem to like that well enough. They asked us to do six more of these things and we decided we would write them all. All the other sort of sketch shows around that time were more or less written by the same people, so we felt that what we had going for us, if we had anything going for us, is it is personal. It is our personal view of the world. It's not a corporate machine that is just generating a sketch from here and a sketch from there.'

To ensure they didn't make the same mistakes as their earlier attempts, they recruited an excellent script editor, Jon Canter, who had previously worked with Mel Smith and Griff Rhys Jones. Jon was also a Cambridge boy and quickly tuned into what the pair were trying to achieve. They also drafted in Roger Ordish, a very experienced director who cut his teeth working with the famous Two Ronnies and also on the *Jim'll Fix It* programme in the 1970s.

Nevertheless, Fry and Laurie knew that having a good producer and director meant nothing unless they had good material to work with. It was their job to step up to the mark.

Fry joked about how tough it was to write all of the material. 'If only there was a manual, telling you who should hold the pen, what colour paper to use.'

'Actually,' confessed Laurie, 'we didn't write any of it. We farmed it out to a Puerto Rican collective in Whitechapel and paid them 60p an hour.' On a serious note, he quickly added, 'But, there is a degree of procrastination when we sit down to write, and some panic too, because we have to come up with three hours of material. You can always write something, but with comedy it has to be something good. Some of the best sketches are finished in 20 minutes, but we spend an awful lot of time thinking of the right names for our characters.'

But behind the humorous wisecracks smokescreen they did

begin to write their own brand of material and wrote it faster and smarter than ever before. They got so good at knocking it out that for the first series they wrote 153 sketches, a lot more than what was actually required. The quantity and quality of the material had improved immensely but some of the sketches were still too long, especially when compared with sketch shows that followed in later years like *The Fast Show* and *Little Britain*.

'We'd set ourselves a hard task,' said Laurie. 'Because we felt that every sketch should be a new one. We had a few repeating things but when we did something we normally wanted to do it once, but then sometimes we went on to long. But we just wrote what came out.'

It was a witty, old fashioned show which highlighted their very own special particular sense of humour and showed that they weren't afraid to try something new. It was a mix of slapstick, clever wordplay and edgy TV innuendos. It forged a comic partnership between them which became one of the strongest and most enduring comedy partnerships in Britain throughout the 1980s and 90s. To add to this mix, Hugh was allowed to demonstrate his musical talents with parodies of musical genres, which he played on the keyboards.

The first series was a success with audiences and critics alike and was similar to the work of Peter Cook and Dudley Moore, to which it was compared. The show seemed to satisfy a section of the British public who had been starved of humour that was intelligent and risqué.

'Stephen is really better at putting himself about. Agreeing to put himself in the firing line,' said Hugh. 'My reaction is always to say, "No, don't do it, you're mad. People will tear you to bits, or they'll think such-and-such about you." He is much more open. He thinks, "Well, that's too bad, but I'll do it anyway."'

A Bit of Fry and Laurie was recorded live in front of a studio audience and proved to be so funny and well received there was never any need to dub in extra laughter. In fact, there is a strong rumour that much of the audience laughter from their show was recorded and used on a number of other BBC comedy shows.

'I've never been aware of being anything big or being famous,' Laurie said, truly surprised at their success, 'but I do look back now and realise that some of the best times were working with Stephen. I just wish I'd been more aware of that then. I worried too much. I made it less enjoyable than it could have been. I'm a worrier by nature and always have been. I worried about failure and not looking an idiot in public.'

A second show was quickly planned. Although Fry and Laurie were more than happy to take advice on things like camera shots and other technical stuff, they, like most writers, weren't too impressed when the director or the producer dared to question some of the material they had written.

'They would both look at you as if...this is not cricket, and were quite resistant if anyone mentioned it,' said writer Jon Canter.

However, Fry and Laurie weren't afraid to continue to learn about the process. They were looking to improve all of the time. Hugh was particularly concerned with feedback from some quarters about the show. 'We realised lots of our stuff was wordy and tended to go on quite a lot. We wanted to find someway of breaking it up.'

After some brainstorming they came up with a way to introduce quick one-off character sketches, very short, very funny and often irrelevant to every thing else going on before and after. They used them to neatly link other sketches and set-pieces. The snippets were typically filmed in some high street, with either of the pair playing normal men-in-the-street while answering insignificant responses to unheard questions. Example were things like, 'They'll be saying Hitler's a racist next' or 'Bring back hanging I say – these tumble-dryers are useless' or Hugh walking out of a shop holding a plate – 'See this...you could eat your dinner off this.' It always produced big laughs from the audience and then it was on to the next sketch.

It may not have been an original concept, in fact it had been used in the *Monty Python* days and the Spike Milligan era, but it was still a very effective solution to the problem of the longer sketches. Laurie explained how they came up with the idea more by accident than design. At the end of the day, tired of the writing process they would often come up with half a sketch or an incomplete sentence which was put to one side for another day. After a while, they started to read through the half-finished sentences and thought that many were quite funny as they were, and so they used them to great effect.

'The typical sketch comes about by one or the other of us taking a line for a walk. M'colleague or I will continue with it on our own for a while, and then yell across the room, "This is arse-wash, see if you can improve it,"' Stephen said.

The main sketches centred on rather conventional styled confrontations between two people in opposing positions of power and authority; in offices, between shop salesman and customer, schoolboy and teacher, and so on. There was never a large budget to work with, but this was used to the duo's advantage. One example was Hugh's interview with pop icon Michael Jackson, who was actually Stephen dressed in normal attire insisting he was Jacko by doing the moonwalk while pacing on a treadmill.

Before the second series aired, Laurie took a giant step forward in his personal life when he married his girlfriend, theatre administrator Jo Green on 16 June 1989 in Camden, London. He says he fell for her because she laughs a lot, and because, he thinks, she likes him, which is great because 'I've gone through a lot of my life thinking that people didn't like me. She is a great administrator. She's got a very good logistical brain. At home we're opposites. I don't answer the phone if I can possibly avoid it and I don't open letters, especially ones in brown envelopes.'

How they ended up together is quite an amusing story – unless you happened to be Hugh's girlfriend at that time. 'My girlfriend was someone called Kate who went away to Kenya to work for a year. I started fooling around with Jo, who had just been left by her boyfriend. It was a pretty squalid episode because the accepted form is that before climbing inside a girl's pants you say "Look, I'm with this other girl, let me go and speak to her." But I didn't, I missed out that stage. So instead of saying, "Kate, it's over. Can I have your assigned chit?" I had to say, "Look, I'm having an affair." Kate was really upset.'

Love, he says, is something he's never been very good at and it is not a word that he uses often. 'Someone repressed like me, with a word like that, goes "steady on!"' He confesses he didn't fall in love often because of the crippling fear of failure. 'I wouldn't approach anyone unless I was fairly sure of success. I struck rarely but accurately.' That all changed with Jo.

They had their first child, Charlie, a year before they got hitched. Fry, who was best man, joked, 'I did try to persuade him against this dizzy course, but Hugh is a great actor who can play at being one of nature's bachelors while himself being one of nature's husbands. I see myself as uncle and advisor to this young couple starting out.'

The marriage didn't alter the writing partners' friendship at all. As a matter of fact, Fry even goes on holidays with the couple on occasions. 'Hugh and his wife Jo are very nice to me and invite me to dinner on Sundays as well as dinner parties. Sad old bachelor…it's nice to have a family to look after you.'

Laurie found that fatherhood gave him a sense of responsibility like nothing else could. He started to drive a sensible car after packing up his beloved motorcycles when he married Jo and when Charlie, an unplanned pregnancy, was six months old. 'As soon as you have a child you think, blimey! One's got to make some proper, er, what I believe are called commitments. There's no point in pretending I'm going to be an 18-year-old gadabout for ever.'

So after the wedding, and with a successful first series in the bag, it was full steam ahead with more TV work. The second series of *A Bit of Fry and Laurie* in 1990 was more consistent, fully rounded and more professional in its appearance. The series made numerous jokes at the expense of the Tory prime ministers of the time, Margaret Thatcher and John Major, with one sketch depicting a televised 'Young Tory of the Year' competition, in which a young Conservative

(Laurie) recites a deliberately incoherent speech consisting only of nonsense political buzzwords, such as 'family values' and 'individual enterprise'.

Director Ordish recalls, 'They had these things in the show that they loved, particularly espionage, the idea of Englishness, corporate England. They absolutely loved taking the piss out of the whole new 80s generation, the red braces wearing group, the Thatcherite people. I think they were ahead of their time.' Maybe it was the effect of working with left-wing socialite Ben Elton for so many years.

While they constantly attacked the yuppie classes, they weren't afraid to venture back to a golden period in British history, like the Edwardian times. Their audiences loved it. The pair, with their upbringing and education, probably suited that style and era more than any other comedy team around at that moment.

Stephen and Hugh's partnership grew stronger and stronger and their writing excelled to new levels. Each episode of the new series began with Stephen and Hugh arriving at the BBC carrying some bizarre items and strutting onto a studio set made up like a badly designed living room. Each episode also featured a musical number from the talented Laurie, which would sometimes feature his partner as well. Fry admitted to being as bad at music as Laurie was good. Fry danced badly, was tone deaf and didn't seem to mind making a complete ass of himself.

Laurie's musical numbers included 'The Polite Rap', a spoof on rap music in which Hugh claims to be a 'good-ass motherliker', an upsetting ode to tennis player Steffi Graf, a rendition of the Beatles' 'Hey Jude' and a bizarre version of

Elvis's 'Love Me Tender'. There were also spoofs of existing TV shows such as *Countdown* and *A Question of Sport*, with the occasional special guest and a mock TV chat-show format.

Everything they tried turned to pure comedy gold, even when they were getting their creative hands slapped for pushing the boundaries too far with sketches including characters like Ted Cunterblast.

'He was a fictional author we created for a Fry and Laurie sketch,' explained a sheepish Laurie. 'And the name got us into a lot of trouble with the controller of BBC Two. He called the producer the next day and said, "They used the word c-u-n-t!" And our producer said, "Well, actually, they used a name, C-u-n-t-erblast." I wouldn't dream of asserting there was anything clever or witty about that, but for some reason it amused our childish selves at the time.'

The third series, in 1992, involved most of the recurring characters, and although it had a larger budget and moments of 'pant-wetting' humour, on the whole it didn't have the edge or the adventure of the previous two. The number of special guests increased, but it lacked original creative material. However, the reviews were still good and the audience viewing figures didn't drop away as many of the rival TV shows had seen at the same stage.

But behind the scenes, things were slowly unravelling. Fry, who had suffered from cyclothymia, a mild form of bipolar disorder, suffered a nervous breakdown in 1995 while appearing in a West End play called *Cell Mates*. After only a few appearances he walked out of the production, causing it to close early and angering co-star Rik Mayall and playwright Simon Gray. After walking out, Fry went missing for several days while contemplating suicide. He then abandoned the idea and left the United Kingdom by ferry, eventually resurfacing in Belgium.

Hugh admits he was slightly miffed that Fry did not call him in his time of crisis, but now he fully understands why. 'He didn't confide in me before he went, which was sort of hurtful at the time. But I kind of know why he didn't, because he knew what I would say which have been something along the lines of "get a hold of yourself man" and you get yourself into a state of mind where you actually don't want to be told.'

When he did finally return, they started on the fourth series, which had been changed from BBC Two to the main flagship channel BBC One. To be given a slot on the main BBC channel was a signal that they had made it to the big time, and they were treated like royalty. Unfortunately, with the timing immediately after Fry's personal problems, the last series in 1995 wasn't considered their best.

Hugh said that the switch to BBC One had nothing to do with them. 'We didn't know it was going to be on BBC One, we made it for Two, but BBC One loved it so much. We really don't know why.' And in usual humble Laurie fashion, he added, 'Perhaps someone died and they had seven half-hour spots to fill.'

The show also had a new director, Bob Spiers, who had worked on *Fawlty Towers*. He loved what the pair had done but wanted some changes including the use of more guests. Laurie didn't really like writing for the guests and preferred the sketch format involving him and Fry. 'It was quite an exercise writing for other people because they could make things work that we didn't imagine working, but also they fuck things up that we couldn't imagine them fucking them up.'

After nine long but successful and fulfilling years, it all ended. In that time, Hugh and Stephen had written and starred in every single sketch in every single show.

'I think they [the BBC] just had enough of us,' Laurie joked. 'We were never really satisfied. We tried our damnedest to get those sketches to work and always felt we never quite made it. Sketches are a young person's thing.'

Stephen was a little more philosophical. 'When you get to the point in your life, get to the age where you could be the teacher, or the judge, or the bishop, or general or MP or whatever, you're not making fun of them in the same way, making fun but less childlike. I suppose by the fourth one we were getting to the age where it was time to pack up the dressing up box and go into the world of acting rather than sketch comedy.'

But the plug being pulled on *A Bit of Fry and Laurie* didn't mean there wasn't life somewhere else. In fact Hugh and Stephen were soon to go on to even greater success.

'He had a wonderfully grave presence. In terms of comedy, he had this miraculous ability to wander onstage, as if it were all a terrible mistake and he belonged somewhere else.'

Stephen Fry

CHAPTER 6

'CANVAS CHAIRS
WITH OUR NAMES
ON THE BACK'

'To be able to write about P.G. Wodehouse is the sort of honour that comes rarely in any man's life, let alone mine.' The excitement was evident in Laurie's voice. 'This is rarity of a rare order. Halley's Comet seems like a blasted nuisance in comparison. If you'd knocked on my head 20 years ago and told me that a time would come when I, Hugh Laurie – scraper-through of O-levels, mover of lips own while reading, loafer, scrounger, pettifogger and general berk of this parish, would be able to carve my initials in the broad bark of the master's oak, I'm pretty certain that I would have said "garn", or something like it.'

That was just one of Hugh's reactions when he, and comedy partner Stephen Fry, were offered the opportunity, an opportunity they had initially refused, to star in a famous piece of work by one of their all-time heroes, P.G. Wodehouse. Sir Pelham Grenville Wodehouse, KBE, was born 15

October 1881 and died 93 years later in 1975, on Long Island, New York. Famously called 'English Literature's Performing Flea', a description Wodehouse used as the title of a collection of his letters to a friend, P.G. Wodehouse is best known for the *Jeeves* and *Blandings Castle* novels and short stories. The name 'Jeeves' comes from Percy Jeeves, a Warwickshire cricketer killed in the First World War. But there was more to Wodehouse than novels: he was also a playwright and lyricist who wrote 15 stage plays and of 250 lyrics for some 30 musical comedies. He worked with Cole Porter on the musical *Anything Goes* (1934) and repeatedly collaborated with Jerome Kern and Guy Bolton. He wrote the lyrics for the hit song 'Bill' in Kern's *Show Boat* (1927), plus he wrote lyrics to Sigmund Romberg's music for Gershwin's *Rosalie* (1928), and collaborated with Rudolf Friml on a musical version of *The Three Musketeers* (1928).

Wodehouse enjoyed enormously popular success during a career of more than 70 years and his prolific writings continue to be widely read. He has been admired both by contemporaries such as Hilaire Belloc, Evelyn Waugh and Rudyard Kipling, and by modern writers such as Douglas Adams, Salman Rushdie, Zadie Smith and Terry Pratchett.

A typical Wodehouse story consists of a light-hearted satirical attack on the British class system, in particular Britain's well-heeled, well-born, empty-headed upper-class twits. Every word he produced is loved by his adoring fans, including the Queen Mother who apparently read the *Jeeves* stories every night before she went to sleep to help put a smile on her face after the strains of the day.

Wodehouse was actually knighted by Queen Elizabeth in

Hugh's father, W.G.R.M 'Ran' Laurie, who was an Olympic gold medallist and, like Hugh, a member of the Cambridge University rowing team.

Above: Hugh with Ben Elton in 1983 comedy sketch show *Alfresco*.

Below: Hugh with (*from left*) Tim McInnerny, Tony Robinson, Rowan Atkinson and Stephen Fry in *Blackadder Goes Forth*, which aired in 1989.

Above: Hugh and Rowan Atkinson signing books at a Comic Relief event in 1989.

Below left: Hugh on stage in *Gasping* at the Theatre Royal, London, in 1990.

Below right: With long-standing comic partner Stephen Fry as Jeeves and Wooster.

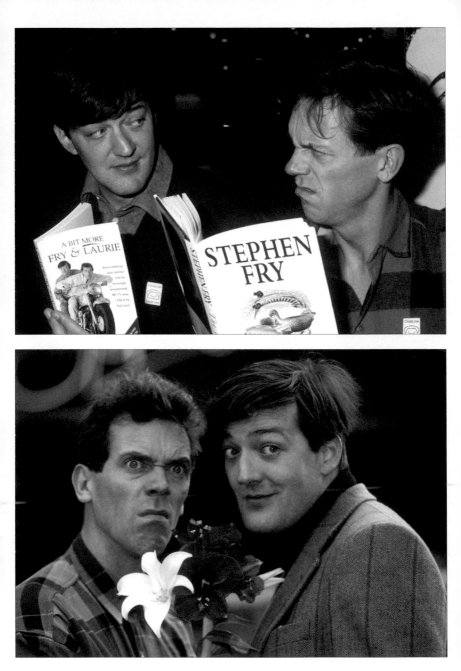

Hugh pictured with Stephen Fry in 1991. Fry and Laurie had an extremely successful career together with *A Bit of Fry and Laurie* and *Jeeves and Wooster* before embarking on equally successful solo projects.

A portrait of Hugh taken in 1992 – proving that he does have the brooding charm of a Hollywood sex symbol, even if he doesn't believe it himself!

Above: Hugh (back row, right) with the cast of *Peter's Friends* in 1992, including Kenneth Branagh, Emma Thompson, Stephen Fry and Tony Slattery.

Below: With Richard E Grant, Juliet Stevenson and Chris Barrie (who got the part of Rimmer in *Red Dwarf*, which Hugh had auditioned for) in *The Legends of Treasure Island*.

Above left: Hugh backstage at the Oxford Playhouse in 1994.

Above right: At a charity cricket match with Julia Carling, who played umpire for the day.

Below: Hugh Laurie and Stephen Fry are still great friends, even though they haven't worked together for many years.

Above: Hugh with co-star Miriam Margolyes on location in Africa for 1997 film *The Place of Lions*.

Below left: Showing his love of cricket again, Hugh takes part in a charity match for Macmillan Cancer Relief in 1999.

Below right: Hugh with Joely Richardson in *Maybe Baby*, the film based on Ben Elton's semi-autobiographical book *Inconceivable*.

1975, even though he had exiled himself in France since the 1940s and was denounced by the British authorities for having made five radio broadcasts of Nazi propaganda during his imprisonment in a comfortable German prison camp when the Second World War broke out in 1939.

As a gifted 11-year-old, Stephen Fry was captivated by the works of the novelist; at the age of 15 he wrote Wodehouse a fan letter and in return received an autographed photo. During the filming of *Jeeves and Wooster*, the photo stood on his dressing-room table as a good-luck charm. 'The greatest pleasure I've ever gained from reading has been from the master, P.G. Wodehouse.'

Hugh Laurie also caught the Wodehouse bug early on in his young life. When assigned to write a school essay about a period in which he would like to have lived, Laurie chose the time brought to life by Wodehouse, the 1920s and 30s. 'I was crestfallen afterwards to be taken aside and told that none of that ever existed,' Laurie said. 'Being told there was no such world was like that ghastly moment when you're told there is no Father Christmas.'

It was Wodehouse's comic genius influence that Laurie said helped him change his own 'squalid' existence. 'I was, in truth, a horrible child. Not much given to things of a booky nature, I spent a large part of my youth smoking Number Six and cheating in French vocabulary tests. I wore platform boots with brass skull and crossbones over the ankle, my hair was disgraceful and I somehow contrived to pull off the gruesome trick of being both fat and thin at the same time. If you had passed me in the street during those pimply years, I am confident that you would, at the very least, have quickened your pace.'

It was no exaggeration either explained Hugh. 'Glancing over my school reports from the year 1972, I observe that the words "ghastly" and "desperate" feature strongly, while "no", "not", "never" and "again" also crop up more often than one would expect in a random sample. My history teacher's report actually took the form of a postcard from Vancouver.'

It all turned out to be a tale of redemption when around his 13th birthday, a copy of his first Wodehouse novel, *Galahad at Blandings*, entered Hugh's foetid world and things quickly began to alter. Reading the opening sentence (while, of course, moving his lips), he felt his life grow larger and larger. 'There had always been height, depth, width and time, and in these prosaic dimensions I had hitherto snarled, cursed, and not washed my hair. But now, suddenly, there was Wodehouse, and the discovery seemed to make me gentler every day. By the middle of the fifth chapter I was able to use a knife and fork, and I like to think that I have made reasonable strides since.'

Fully immersed in this imaginary world, Hugh spent the next few years wandering aimlessly back and forth through the book of Blandings Castle and its surroundings. He knew everything there was about each story, about each character. He even learned how often the trains ran in Wodehouse world and at what times the post was collected. He could tell if the Empress was off-colour and knew why the Emsworth Arms was preferable to the Blue Boar; all the things that really mattered in the life of an impressionable young boy of that age. Then into his teens, he opened up his first *Jeeves* novel and without a second thought he dived head first inside, and has been swimming among the warm friendly pages every since.

'The facts in this case, ladies and gentlemen, are simple. The first thing you should know, and probably the last, too, is that P.G. Wodehouse is still the funniest writer ever to have put words on paper. Fact number two: with the Jeeves stories, Wodehouse created the best of the best. I speak as one whose first love was Blandings and who later took immense pleasure from P Smith, but Jeeves is the jewel, and anyone who tries to tell you different can be shown the door, the mini-cab, the train station, and Terminal 4 at Heathrow with a clear conscience. The world of Jeeves is complete and integral, every bit as structured, layered, ordered, complex and self-contained as King Lear, and considerably funnier.

'Of course Jeeves and Wooster in the books are fabulous characters, but they are characters in a fairly superficial sense. The real star of the thing is the language and the beauty of it is the way the language just sort of skates, almost as if it were verse. You can't afford to take too much time about naturalism, really. The sentences are so beautifully constructed you want to hear them ping through in one go, without someone breaking it and doing a naturalistic um and an er and staring at the ceiling.'

The stories of Jeeves are set in Britain and the United States during the pre-Second World War period of the 1920s and 30s. Throughout the books clueless socialite, Bertie Wooster, who is rich, single, kind-hearted and fun-loving, can't help himself from getting into scrapes; his life is filled with dangers.

'Bertie is not really a fool, although he does some pretty

foolish things, but only from the motive of wanting to do the best, to get people out of a jam. He is such a good soul,' said Laurie. 'His whole aim in life is to help his idiot friends out of trouble, and he really has no thought of self. You can imagine that he'd be very good company. His use of language is so fabulous that just asking you if you'd like a cup of tea would become an event.'

Coming to Bertie's rescue on a day-to-day basis is his manservant, Jeeves, who as well as organising his master's clothes, food, diary and supporting his leisure hours, sees trouble before it happens and is nearly always ready with advice.

'Everyone would like to have a Jeeves. He is not really a servant and he can't be because we would all be embarrassed by having a butler,' Fry commented. 'We wouldn't know how to talk to him. It really goes back to *Aladdin*, with Jeeves as the genie. The genie could always mock his master.'

Hugh Laurie concluded, 'Jeeves is the guide, philosopher and friend everyone needs. The nanny to put you to bed at night and make sure you are comfortable.'

Wodehouse drew the themes of his plots, which concerned the entangled love lives of the major characters, from classical new comedy. The dramas are filled with lots of other eccentric's characters throughout the stories. Gussie Fink-Nottle is obsessed by newts; Archibald Mulliner adores socks; Mr Anstruther is the 'wettest man in Worcestershire'; Tuppy Glossop is a fun-loving fool. Sir Watkyn Bassett, the owner of Totleigh Towers, is the father of Madeline; Madeline Bassett is a hopeless romantic and Jeeves is determined to stop her from becoming engaged to his master.

Among other things, Madeline believes that every time a fairy blows its nose a child is born.

Down the years, there have been a couple of attempts to translate Wodehouse onto television, including a few adaptations of the Jeeves stories. The last was *The World of Wooster* on the BBC (1965–67), which starred Ian Carmichael as Wooster and Dennis Price as Jeeves. Twenty-three years later, in 1990, Granada in association with Picture Partnership Productions decided it was time to revive the novels again, and they didn't hide the fact that they really wanted Hugh and Stephen to play the main roles of Bertie Wooster and Jeeves respectively.

When they were originally offered the roles of the master and manservant, these two admirers of Wodehouse thought it best to decline because they were too afraid of antagonizing the millions of other fans all over the world, each of whom already knew precisely how the characters should look and sound.

Laurie explains exactly why they considered not pursuing the opportunity. 'Actually, we nearly turned it down.' He paused. 'We sort of did turn it down because we thought it was an impossible thing to achieve. Among a certain class of British life. Both of us had the immediate reaction, "This can't be done, you can't do it and not only can't you do it, you're playing with a delicate porcelain figure and we are going to break it."' Laurie continues, 'Yes, and if you muck it up, you really are in such trouble, because one knows what Wodehouse adorers are like. Lots of these people who like Wodehouse are a bit mad. It's a religion for them. They live it and if you don't come up to scratch they let you know. They all have an image of Jeeves' and Wooster's world in their heads, and there is always the possibility that anybody who plays them might ruin that image.'

Understandably upset, the producers decided to move on in search of two other actors to play the parts. By then Fry and Laurie were already having second thoughts, especially when Hugh read the scripts from start to finish in one afternoon, which he normally doesn't do because he believes most scripts are generally dull things to read. 'I just read it in one sitting and I laughed all the way through it. There was some really great stuff and so I rang up Stephen and said, "Wait, don't say no yet."'

Fry picks up the narrative. 'Part of the reason we thought we could say no is that the books are written by Bertie, as it were, in the first person. And he describes Jeeves, for instance, as, y'know, his feet don't touch the floor, he shimmers into rooms, he oozes out of rooms. He seems to flicker and then he isn't there. He coughs and it's like a sheep clearing its throat of a blade of grass on a distant hillside or something. I tried practising that but sounded more like a goat clearing its throat of a piece of cheese on a nearby hillside. These things are difficult.'

But Fry knew they should at least try it and so they phoned the producers back and grovelled a little. 'I said to them, "When we said no, we really meant yes," before adding, "Look if anyone is going to bugger this up it's going to be us, thank you very much."'

The difficult task of translating the stories from the printed page to a television script fell to Clive Exton, who succeeded beautifully in capturing the charm and humour. One of

Exton's tricks was to combine several stories to make up one episode.

Fry stated, 'The scripts were like an antiseptic cream. They were so gracefully done, capturing all of Bertie Wooster's enchanting language. Theirs is a wonderful world that one just wants to dive into, like being able to dive into a soufflé.'

Within a few months of finally saying yes, Hugh found himself slipping into a double-breasted suit in a Prince of Wales check pattern while Fry made himself at home inside an enormous bowler hat. 'And the two of us embarked on our separate disciplines; him for the noiseless opening of decanters, me for the twirling of the whangee [umbrella].'

Although there was some doubt among members of the Wodehouse Society about their appropriateness for such honoured parts, Fry and Laurie proved without a shadow of a doubt that they were simply perfect in the roles of unsurpassable valet Jeeves and 'bally ass' Wooster, living in a 1920s–30s world of Hooray Henries and marvellously stubborn aunts.

The first series of five episodes was shown in the spring of 1990, and it ran for another three years up until 1993 to general critical acclaim. It was important to keep the TV series as faithful to the books as possible. The biggest single decision was taking away the narrator, which may have upset the purist, but Hugh believes was necessary for the series to work on TV. 'The spirit of the thing, I hope, is as faithful as it is as possible to get. So the great P.G. was making his presence felt in my life once more. And I soon learnt that I still had much to learn. How to smoke plain cigarettes, how to drive a 1927 Aston Martin, how to mix a Martini with five parts water and one part water for filming purposes only, how to attach a pair of spats in less than a day and a half, and so on.' He added, 'I feel a charlatan, having been given those wonderful scripts. It is often the way that the things others like are those that cost you the least. It just seems too easy.'

While purists of Wodehouse would understandably point out that there was too much mucking about with storylines, or that Stephen Fry was perhaps too young to play Jeeves, the show was a success because the performances were outstanding, the production lavish, the music fun, and the writing captured much of the language that makes Wodehouse such a joy to read. The series was responsible for introducing countless new fans to the work of P.G. Wodehouse and the series remains a classic.

During interviews about the first series, the pair were often asked if there was any talk of role reversal, with Fry playing Bertie Wooster, the jovial but empty-headed young gentleman, and Laurie as Jeeves, his improbably well-informed and talented valet.

'No, not really,' said Laurie. 'I suppose it had to be this way round because of the voice. I have a sort of sickly green voice.'

'I have a dark brown voice. A Jeeves voice,' added Fry. 'Also Hugh does have the look of a Bertie Wooster. Those big green eyes...and that air of innocence. And I look older. Jeeves has perhaps only a few years over Bertie but...well, you really can tell a lot about a person from the way he brushes his teeth. When Bertie brushes his teeth he looks like a schoolboy, not a grown up. I'm certainly not adroit, efficient, neat, quiet on my feet and respectful like Jeeves. On the other hand, I do tend to remember quotations and regurgitate facts like him.'

However, Fry claimed he tried purposely 'not' to play Jeeves quite as loftily as Dennis Price, who played the role in the televised adaptation more than 20 years previously. 'Price was equipped with a fairly astonishing pair of eyebrows and they were what made the character somewhat smug. I think I have made Jeeves more respectful, just as Hugh has made Bertie Wooster less of a yammering ass than Ian Carmichael made him in that series.'

'One hopes,' added Laurie, 'that people watch it because it is funny. P.G. Wodehouse was arguably the greatest comic writer who ever lived, I think. But in England a lot of the audience are watching it not because of the drama but because of the setting, "Oh, I love those old clothes, they're all double-breasted suits, and those cars, so lovely with the big curves and chrome bumpers, and the big, lovely houses." Because it's a taste of a kind of Garden of Eden that never really existed in England, or if it did, it wasn't on the scale that's suggested in Wodehouse. You can argue that it's an unhealthy facet, and I'm afraid it's our fault!'

In real life, Stephen believed the both of them were probably the complete opposite to the characters they had been chosen to play in the series. 'Hugh is the practical one and sensible about things. And I'm vaguer and vacillatory, which sounds like some kind of lubricate.'

Hugh chipped in, 'Obviously, and Stephen's got a better vocabulary,' he joked.

All in all, Hugh loved everything about the experience, from the scripts to the sets, to the locations. 'I enjoyed playing the part,' Hugh joked. 'We had canvas chairs with our names on the back.' Yet strangely Hugh found the funny parts most difficult and more worrisome than anything else, he was afraid the words were so precious that he would break or destroy them.

During the first series, the actors became aware quite quickly that the action was bordering on the slow side. They were conscious that many costume dramas were immensely sluggish and drawn out and they felt a need to add some pace to the proceedings. So to ensure they kept up the beat, they wrote the word 'PACE' on the back of the clapboard to remind all of them at the beginning of every shot.

'My theory,' Hugh said, 'is that because it's in those older days, the actors were wearing more or less contemporary clothes, and that if you put actors in period clothes now, they talk slower maybe because they feel less comfortable and more awkward. You put modern women in big hats and fur coats and brooches and gloves and handbags and all this gear, and therefore they feel more self-conscious and more obliged to give a stately sort of reading.'

Fry realised there was a strong desire to get the pace right. 'Whereas with comedy of this kind, one thinks of recapturing the pacing of those great movies of the '30s and '40s, the Capras and the Preston Sturgeses and the speed of Cary Grant going rat-a-tat-tat. A 1930s screenplay would probably be twice as many pages as a '90s screenplay. They just go at it at a heck of a lick.'

Even with all the hard work there was still time for some fun. In between filming, Hugh and Stephen made use of wasted time by performing magic tricks they took from a book. 'And which we did badly,' joked Laurie.

The crew themselves also got into character. 'When

shooting,' said Laurie, 'the crew, who I wouldn't say are fouled mouthed but have their own rich Anglo-Saxon way of putting things, would often take on the Wodehouse language. When a big tattooed scene shifter dropped something like a spanner on their foot, they would say, "Oh heck! Or "dash it." Of course there are no swear words in Wodehouse. "Oh heck" is the strongest you get. And only a couple of hecks in each show; we don't want people to phone in and complain,' he joked. 'In Wodehouse world, the bedroom is a place where Jeeves delivers tea, that's all. It is all innocence.'

The reviews for the first series, and in fact the entire series, were extremely positive. 'Clive Exton does seem to have kept a period feel without consigning them entirely to a long-gone age, and that suits the work of Hugh Laurie and Stephen Fry who manage to keep the humour modern enough to laugh at. This is the job Fry and Laurie's partnership might have been born for,' wrote Patrick Stoddart of *The Sunday Times*.

Peter Porter, *The Times Literary Supplement* reviewer, wrote, 'The director and his actors must be given the major share of the credit, especially Hugh Laurie as Wooster. From the moment we first see him nursing a hangover in the dock after a Boat Race jape of stealing a policeman's helmet, we are conducted along a switchback of facial expressions that lifts the personality of Wooster onto a different plane from any representation of him filmed before.'

During the second series, and while halfway through filming one of the episodes, Hugh's second child was born. 'Bill was born in the middle of a scene, actually. I was still in costume when the phone rang and I dashed to the hospital and wallop, three o'clock there he was.' Stephen had to do rest of the scene pretending to be talking to Hugh while talking to thin air. He became Bill's godfather, as he is to Hugh's other son, Charlie.

Another two series were produced after the first two, making it four in all, with a total of 23 episodes across the entire run. Hugh enjoyed every minute of it and strangely found himself relating to the character more and more. 'I went to a very nobby school and saw some pretty crusty figures. Bertie Wooster is about a certain kind of gormlessness, which tends to overcome me when I'm nervous.'

In the last series, Jeeves and Wooster spread their wings and headed off to New York for several episodes; well, not exactly New York but Pinewood studios in Buckinghamshire which was duly transformed into the city that never sleeps. In a twist to the series they venture out in the country to explore rodeos, roller derbies and racoon coats.

'Bertie takes to America like a duck to water, said Laurie. 'Jeeves, of course, disapproves.'

So, after three years, four series and over 23 episodes, *Jeeves and Wooster* ended, to the great sadness of its loyal viewers in the UK and other parts of the world.

'It was great fun to do,' said Laurie, 'but very expensive, with the lavish cars, suits, dresses and country houses. Also we ran through the plots so quickly. We would do a novel in about an hour. After about 23 hours of it…we had done Wodehouse. By the third series you do notice that old Wodehouse, bless him, does let the same plot, even the same scenes, crop up. But there's always at least one line that is a physical pleasure to say. It's ingenious.'

Fry was also extremely pleased with the outcome of *Jeeves and Wooster*. 'It was Sunday evening television at its best in the sense that it was like dropping yourself into a great soufflé with the cars, the ashtrays, the cocktail shakers, the hairstyles, the silliness, the language, the characterisation, the locations. Everything about it was charming and British.'

And like Hugh, Fry also believes they probably shot their bolt in those 23 hours. 'I know it isn't much compared to an American series, that if successful, goes on for 11 years, like *Cheers* or something. But for a start, we're limited by the amount of stories P.G. Wodehouse told, because I don't think his estate, which is still active, would relish the idea of brand-new stories being made up.'

There was talk about the possibility of a stage play based on a couple of the stories, but everyone thought it seemed like a cheap way of cashing in on something that they had already done for four years. 'John Cleese is convinced,' said Fry, 'that we should do a movie, which I find utterly incomprehensible. But for television, anyhow, there's the limitation of the number of stories to start with, and also just a feeling, I suppose, on our part that we don't want to be too identified with those roles and each of us is working on our own things.'

Commenting on the show's ending, Hugh shrugged his shoulders. 'Unfortunately *Jeeves and Wooster* is history, I'm afraid. It did not do quite as well in the US as we had hoped. Also, I started to go bald. I don't really know what happened to Bertie, but at some point I had to bow out of the role.'

More thoughtfully, he added, 'Naturally, one hopes there were compensations in watching Wodehouse on the screen, pleasant scenery, amusing clothes, a particular actor's eyebrows, but it can never replicate the experience of reading him. If I may go slightly culinary for a moment, a dish of foie gras nestling on a bed of truffles, with a side-order of lobster and caviar may provide you with a wonderful sensation, but no matter how wonderful, you simply don't want to be spoon-fed the stuff by a perfect stranger. You need to hold the spoon, and decide for yourself when to wolf and when to nibble. And so I am back to reading, rather than playing Jeeves. And my Wodehousian redemption is, I hope, complete. Indeed, there is nothing left for me to say, except to wish, as I fold away my penknife and gaze up at the huge oak towering overhead, that my history teacher could see me now.'

So, after so much time together, it was the right moment for a break for the two hard-working actors. The pair had spent eight solid months together, three months writing and two months filming *A Bit of Fry and Laurie*, and then, straight after, another three months on *Jeeves and Wooster*.

The show finished and the two moved on. Hugh was quite hopeful they would work together again. 'We often talk about it but we will probably go to our graves talking about it like two old duffers. I certainly hope so. We're not very good at planning, to be honest, we don't have a Sasco year planner, which is something we keep meaning to get, with the month written on it so we can say, "Invade Poland in February". We just bumble along without ever really planning what we're going to do, although he is directing his first film this autumn and if I don't get a part in that there are going to be some pretty sharp questions asked! So I hope to be working with him pretty soon.'

'Once, when we were filming *Jeeves and Wooster* there was a long delay as technicians adjusted light reflectors. Hugh Laurie kindly tried to keep me amused by offering to show me how to play the castanets with spoons. I told him gravely that I'd rather not, thank you. I was trying to "focus".'

Hermione Eyre, who played Clementina in
Jeeves and Wooster

PART 2

LOSING HUGH'S VIRGINITY BUT FINDING LAURIE'S MIND

CHAPTER 7

'I GOT MY COAT TRAPPED IN A CAR DOOR'

'I hope I don't spend my entire life pulling silly faces and saying, "By Jove." But perhaps I will.' Hugh began to feel the need to shed his bumbling upper-class fool, Bertie Wooster's, skin and stretch himself in a new direction. 'Something tortured and profound would be a big challenge.'

After the tremendous success of Hugh and Stephen's TV adventures, the pair continued to work together but not in anything as intense or as time-consuming as they had done before. They did a benefit show for Amnesty International called *The Secret Policeman's Third Ball* as well as the charity stage events, *Hysteria III*, Comic Relief, and *Fry and Laurie Host a Christmas Night with the Stars* in 1994.

Predictably, there wasn't a shortage of job offers on the table for Hugh when the P.G. Wodehouse series finished. As a household name with a very recognisable voice, Hugh has found regular voiceover work in at least 18 high-profile TV commercials over the years, including Fisher-Price, Energizer batteries and Walker's crisps. He actually appeared in person in some others including advertisements for Kellogg's, Bradford & Bingley, Marks & Spencer and Alliance & Leicester to name just a few. Maybe not the most taxing of work for an actor looking to stretch himself, but it proved to be an easy and extremely lucrative way to help keep the wolves from the door.

One avenue Hugh did refuse to return to was the stage. 'I've only done one professional play and that was enough,' Hugh grunted after completing his first 'proper' stage play at the Theatre Royal Haymarket in London's West End in 1990. Even though by then he was more than accustomed to getting up on stage to perform in front of hundreds of people, it was an experience he felt uneasy with. 'I remember a very strange thing happened to me when I started doing it professionally. Up till that point, as a teenager doing school plays and amateur dramatic stuff, I'd always thought of the audience as being female. I don't mean made up of women. I mean in its character, an audience was female. An audience was a thing to be sort of flirted with or seduced in some way, and there was a sort of exciting flirtation between the performer and the audience.' That changed once he went pro. 'The audience almost instantly became male in my head. And all I could picture was this big lump of an audience as a group of very sullen-looking blokes with arms folded as if to say, "Okay, then. Whaddya got?" The audience was something that had to be beaten.'

In the play, Hugh took on the role of Philip, a fast-talking car-salesman type of character with slicked back hair in Ben 'the one-man writing machine' Elton's first stage play, which was based on his best selling novel, *Gasping*.

The ex-Cambridge Blue shivered at the thought of 'how the hell they managed to pull it off'. 'Ben Elton had never written a West End play before. I'd never starred in one and the director (Youssef El-Gingihy) had never directed one before either.' It was a recipe one would have thought had disaster written all over it. However, although the production had an inexperienced cast, few props and hardly any music, it surprisingly worked. But was it ever in doubt? As with most things written by Elton, *Gasping*'s strong dialogue surrounded a fascinating plot of exaggerated corporate life with subtle references and satirical humour. It was that, mixed with excellent acting, which brought Elton's vision to the stage quite delightfully.

The concept of the play focused on the cutthroat world of corporate business and the materialistic yuppie generation. Sir Chiffley Lockheart of Lockheart Industries, played brilliantly by Bernard Hill, who came to prominence as Yosser Hughes in the cult TV show *The Boys from the Black Stuff*, is looking for a new way to make a stack of money. Philip (Hugh), his number two, suggests selling 'designer air' under the banner of 'Perrier for the nostrils'. Incredibly, it takes off and millions of pounds are quickly made for the gluttonous Lockheart. Until greed takes over and the world gets divided into people who can afford it and those who are left 'gasping' for air to survive.

As a matter of fact, the experience almost left Laurie himself breathless as the curtains went up on opening night. Hugh admitted to genuinely thinking he was going to pass out right there on the stage. 'As well as all the usual nerves, butterflies in the stomach, shaking a bit, breathing quickly, trembling knees, inability to swallow, I was almost hallucinating and things were starting to spin.' At one stage during the night he swore it felt as if he was having an out of body experience as he imagined himself floating above the stage looking down on the action.

'Most frightening of all was that for my character, once the play had started, there was no moment in the whole of the first half to get my breath,' he said. 'I shouted all through the first act, then was back on again. By the end I longed for a play where I could lie on a sofa in a dressing gown with a glass of cold tea and gently talk and stare at the ceiling.'

As expected, Hugh was as pessimistic as ever about his performance, but the audience and the critics pictured it quite differently and despite the rawness of everyone involved in the production the reviews were very good. The *Independent* said, 'A sharp-witted satire on the heartlessness of market forces...extremely funny...it never, unlike the world's population, runs out of puff, with a stunning performance from Hugh Laurie as a corporate yes-man who finally sees the light.'

The show ran for several successful weeks, and although excited and pleased to be given the opportunity to tread the boards, by the end of the run he admitted it nearly drove him around the bend. The monotony of doing the same thing every night made him lose his mind on more than one occasion, and he swore it was something he would never do again.

'Eight times a week doing the same thing, standing in the same position, I thought I was going crazy. The guy who played the same character in *Cats* for 16 years, I don't get that.'

On the other side of the fence, Elton loved the experience so much so that he went on to write many other successful stage plays based on his novels including *Silly Cow* (1991) and *Popcorn* (1996). *Popcorn* won the TMA Barclays Theatre Award for Best New Play and the Olivier Award for Best Comedy. In France, the production of *Popcorn* ran for a year in Paris and was nominated for seven Molicre Awards. In 1998 Ben's play *Blast from the Past* played a record-breaking season at the West Yorkshire Playhouse.

With a career on the West End or Broadway out of the question, and without his sidekick partner, Hugh spent the next decade, according to him, wandering aimlessly around between the world of TV and movie-land and back again, with the odd diversion to do a spot of writing along the way.

'My career is a mess,' he said around that time. 'There is no coherence, no plan and no drive. I just blunder from one part to the next. My goal? I'm still looking for it.'

Despite not having a firm plan written on the back of a cigarette packet, never mind carved in stone, a series of high-profile films and TV shows followed as Hugh found himself playing opposite some of the world's biggest actors and actresses in roles involving small rodents, girl-powered pop stars and little people who lived under the floorboards, plus many others.

It turned out to be a busy and demanding couple of years.

First, Hugh travelled to the beautiful city of Prague to play the dissident uncle of a seven-year-old girl in a complex political film called *The Pin for the Butterfly*. It was an unusually serious role for Hugh as the movie focused on the life and struggles of a small bourgeois family living in Stalinist Czechoslovakia in the 1950s. Packed to the rafters with very respectable British character actors, such as Joan Plowright, Ian Bannen and Imogen Stubbs, the film concentrates on the innocent viewpoint of a little girl, Marushka, played by Florence Hoath, in the face of war, and how with the help of her uncle she decides to try to escape the country.

Hugh's role in the film proved to be a quite a test and reviews on his performance were mixed. There were many who said he pulled it off quite skilfully, while there were an equal number who stated he looked quite uneasy getting to grips with the serious role of the revolutionary uncle.

It didn't deter him, however, and he moved onto another film which, in reality, could have been written about Hugh and his Footlights' mates, most of whom, including Stephen Fry, also starred in the movie. *Peter's Friends*, released in 1992, is a British comedy-drama film which was written in five days by Rita Rudner and her husband Martin Bergmann (who had also been in the Footlights while at college). The original screenplay, aimed principally at the American market, had been written with an all-American cast in mind, but a transatlantic version became necessary when Kenneth Branagh signed on to direct and produce the film.

Peter's Friends is about a group of old mates from university who get together ten years after graduation. Peter, played by Stephen Fry, inherits a large estate from his recently deceased father and invites the rest of the gang to spend the New Year's holiday with him where he plans to reveal a shocking secret. Besides directing, Kenneth Branagh also has a role in the film as a Hollywood writer with a loud American wife (Rita Rudner). Laurie plays a quiet old soul who writes jingles for adverts; he is married to Imelda Staunton. Alphonsia

Emmanuel pops up as a glamorous costume designer and Emma Thompson, who was married to Branagh at the time, plays Maggie, an eccentric who works in publishing. Another old Footlights member, Tony Slattery, was cast as the uncouth boyfriend of Alphonsia, while Phyllida Law, Emma's real-life mother, plays Peter's disapproving housekeeper, Vera.

Often compared to the movie *The Big Chill* because both feature friends getting together to catch up on the past, it is primarily a comedy with a twist. It touches on some sombre themes such as friendship, marriage, fidelity and coping with death. Like the majority of films produced around that time, it also played out to a first-rate soundtrack which featured songs by big hitters such as Springsteen, Clapton, The Pretenders and Tears for Fears.

On playing Roger, a man finding it difficult to express his true feelings until suddenly forced to do so, Hugh said, 'I tend only to take on work I know I can do. But with this film I got into something, emotionally, that was out of my depth and, er, well, it turned out better than I'd hoped.' He added that working with Imelda Staunton helped him get through some tough scenes. 'I was really lucky to be doing it with her. It was like I got my coat trapped in a car door and got dragged along because she was so good.'

Although the film proved a major success for all of the ex-Footlights members, Hugh began to have doubts as to whether stardom was the type of life he really wanted as all the attention of being in the public spotlight began to sit uncomfortably on his broad shoulders. 'Being recognised in the supermarket is absolutely hellish and not why I went into the business.' He began to search deep inside of himself.

'I am terribly conscious of the fact that the world doesn't need any more actors. There are so many brilliant actors around that one more twit like me joining the back of the queue seems completely unnecessary.' It also concerned him that he didn't have what it took to carry it off. 'I don't know how actors do it. I was spellbound watching *Coronation Street* when Don and Ivy were close to splitting up. I'm amazed by actors who can cry. I'd have to get a stunt man to do the emotional stuff. But I'd be perfectly happy to do the car crashes myself.'

While internally he struggled with success, outwardly he found himself reaching into his ever-growing bag of different personalities to play Leo Hopkins, a con-man and gambler, in a compelling TV story of a modern-day man who plays dangerous games with other people's money, with catastrophic and fatal results.

All or Nothing at All, in 1993, was written by Guy Andrews, co-creator and co-writer of the series *Chancer*. The mini-series, originally shown in three parts on the UK's ITV network, featured Hugh as a horrifying, convincing, yet charming man who has everything: a successful career as a financial market analyst, a beautiful wife, fine children, two homes and good friends – until he gambles it all with tragic consequences.

'Leo is flawed, my God he's flawed,' Hugh commented on his character. 'He brings untold misery to those who love him. But unless he was lovable it would be like watching someone breaking car aerials all the way down the street. You wouldn't care what happened to him.'

In the series, Hugh stars alongside one of Britain's iconic

stand-up comedians, and TV presenter, Bob Monkhouse, as his boss, Giles.

The director, Andrew Grieve, described the drama as 'A three-hour descent into the hell of a life ruined by an addiction. But this is not an addiction to drugs or love or power. It's the addiction to danger, to putting yourself on the edge.'

To fully immerse himself into character, Hugh tried his hand at something he rarely thought twice about, gambling. 'My first outing into gambling was very successful. Like a mug, I thought it was great and went back for more. I could have been done for, like Leo. Hitting a good patch early on can be fatal.'

The positive reaction he received from portraying such a serious character whetted his appetite for more serious roles; if only for the short term. 'But making people laugh is what I've always wanted to do. Besides, I don't think I'll ever see myself as a proper actor, or escape the feeling that so many people out there can do it better than I can.'

How wrong could the man destined to play the star in one of the most popular American dramas have been?

But even back then, they were unwarranted words indeed for a man about to walk into one of the biggest romantic period dramas of the 1990s. The romantic books of British novelist Jane Austen were proving to be all the rage as a string of them were made into successful movies. A film adaptation of *Persuasion* won critical claim earlier in 1995, while the modernised version of *Emma* entitled *Clueless*, introduced a brand new younger audience to Austen's storytelling and made Alicia Silverstone a star the same year. A television series of *Pride and Prejudice*, starring Colin Firth, was also a worldwide hit. Yet it was *Sense and Sensibility*, Austen's often forgotten first novel, which became her greatest hit in 1995. Not only did the film make more than 100 top 10 best movie lists, but it thrust Kate Winslet into the dizzying heights of superstardom and made Emma Thompson the first person ever to receive an Oscar for both acting (*Howard's End* in 1992) and writing (*Sense and Sensibility* in 1995).

Producer Lindsay Doran, who had previously worked on *This Is Spinal Tap* (1984) and *Ghost* (1990), was the driving focus behind turning the book by Austen into a movie after falling in love with the story while living briefly in England in the 1970s. It took her 20-odd years to work her way through the ranks as a producer before she finally got the chance to make the film she had dreamt about. The next thing was finding someone to write the screenplay. All the pieces fell neatly into place when she was working on *Dead Again* (1991), which co-starred Kenneth Branagh and Emma Thompson. On the set, Thompson's wit caught Doran's attention and she was hugely impressed with what the English actress had written on her own sketch comedy TV series *Thompson*, aired in the United States. Doran believed she had found someone more than qualified to adapt *Sense and Sensibility* to the screen.

Thompson spent the next four and a half years working on the screenplay, going through endless scripts and revisions of the story. Apparently the first draft of the screenplay consisted of 350 handwritten pages and then it took her another 13 drafts before it was ready. During that time, disaster nearly struck when Emma confessed to losing the final version of the screenplay on her faulty computer. She panicked when the computer repairman could not retrieve the file, and in a daze she hailed a cab and took the computer to her old friends Fry and Laurie, who shared a flat together. Fry, in particular, spent seven hours on the job until the missing file was safely retrieved.

When finally finished, the screenplay remained reasonably authentic to the spirit of the book, while Thompson managed to plug a few gaps in the original story and also add a bit of light humour throughout. The main focus was as much on the relationship between the two older Dashwood sisters as on their romantic dreams.

During casting, Emma hoped Doran would select real-life sisters Natasha and Joely Richardson, the daughters of Vanessa Redgrave, for the two main roles. Meanwhile, producer Doran offered the job of directing the movie to Taiwan-based director Ang Lee. It seemed an odd choice since Lee had never even read a Jane Austen novel when Columbia first sent him the script, but Doran was more than confident after seeing the work he had done with the complicated relationships in *The Wedding Banquet* (1993) and *Eat Drink Man Woman* (1994). It was that kind of style Doran wanted for her movie.

Anxious to make his mark immediately, Lee made several suggestions about replacing lengthy dialogue-led scenes with more visual shoots. He also proposed that Thompson play the older sister, Elinor. Thompson strongly disagreed because she felt that at 36, she was way too old to play a role of a 19-year-old. Adamant, Lee suggested increasing Elinor's age to 27, which would make her more believable to the audiences as a spinster.

When Thompson began to write the screenplay, she had Hugh Grant firmly in her mind for the role of Edward. The floppy-haired English star agreed to play the role and since the budget for the film was only $15 million, he also agreed to do it for a much lower fee then he would usually command. With the cast coming together nicely, the only problem was finding the right actress for Elinor's younger, more romantic sister, Marianne. Rumours had it that Kate Winslet really wanted to star in the role, but was only being considered in a supporting part because Lee was less than impressed with her work in the film *Heavenly Creatures* in 1994. However Kate wasn't in the mood to be overlooked and she marched into the room at the audition claiming her agent told her she was reading for Marianne's part; like a girl on a mission, she nailed the role and was offered the job after a single reading.

With Emma, Hugh Grant and Kate Winslet on board, it was not surprising to find out that the rest of the supporting cast assembled were also straight out of the top drawer of method actors. Alan Rickman, with a stack of villainous roles behind him, showed he was just as comfortable in a romantic part as Colonel Brandon. Veteran Gemma Jones slotted in perfectly as Mrs Dashwood. Laurie played the role of Mr Palmer, the disillusioned husband of a silly wife.

Emma Thompson later wrote in her published diary of the filming, 'There is no one on the planet who could capture Mr Palmer's disenchantment and redemption so perfectly, and could make it so funny.'

Like lots of film of this size, *Sense and Sensibility* had its fair share of issues when filming started. One of the largest was the trouble Director Lee had adjusting to the Western approach to film-making. In particular, he would lose his temper, screaming out in Chinese when anyone dared to question his way of directing; back in Taiwan, no one dared to question anything he did. But this was England and many of the British cast had worked on bigger films, with bigger directors, where they were often encouraged to get involved in all aspects of the production. It proved to be a clash of styles and cultures with the director's authoritarian approach upsetting the actors and in turn causing Hugh Grant to apparently call him 'The Brute', but not to his face. The feuding deepened when Lee seemed determined to have Grant deliver a performance unlike anything he had done before.

But as demanding and difficult as Lee could be, he did a great job of bringing a much deeper meaning to the film by insisting the actors use some unusual techniques to feel the emotion of the period drama. He had Winslet read novels and poetry from the era and then report back to him to ensure she fully understood her character's romantic side. Since letter writing was the principal means of communication in Austen's day, he also asked the actors to write letters to each other in character.

Perhaps his shrewdest move was getting Winslet and Thompson to room together so they could develop a real sisterly bond. At the time, both of the women were going through painful breakups: Winslet with her boyfriend and Thompson from her husband, Kenneth Branagh. The plan worked and the two actresses got on like a house on fire. In fact, they remain friends to this day.

There were other issues besides Lee's temper to be resolved. The Jane Austen Society telephoned co-producer James Schamus to complain about the casting of Hugh Grant, claiming that he was too good-looking to play Edward Ferrars. Then there were the sheep. In one sequence, a flock of sheep proved difficult when they wouldn't do what they were told; others keeled over due to the heat and their heavy wool coats. They were promptly sheared and later appeared with their haircuts despite the wintry setting. And the sheep weren't the only difficult animals. One horse had a bout of flatulence so noisy and frequent that the sounds had to be edited out of the soundtrack later on. An angry Ang Lee swore that he would never again use animals on a movie set. However ten years later, the director actually won an Oscar for the film *Brokeback Mountain* – which is about two men who meet while sheep herding.

Despite the farting horses, fainting sheep and grumpy director, it wasn't all doom and gloom on the set. There was some time for fun among the cast and crew. In between filming, although Laurie did his best to spend some quality time alone in his trailer writing his first novel, he did occasionally venture out, and entertained everyone by playing the blues on his guitar along with Greg Wise. He was also presented with the imaginative award for maintaining his composure in a very embarrassing moment: during filming, he kept treading on the train of Imelda's dress, pulling it down so far that on more than one occasion, it exposed her boobs.

All in all, whatever Lee did, it worked. *Sense and Sensibility* was a surprise hit, bringing in $135 million worldwide on its small budget. One of the dominant films when award season came around, with Emma winning her Oscar for Best Adapted Screenplay, the film received six other Academy nominations including Best Picture. The film won three Bafta awards including Best Film and Best Actress for Emma. The movie also won two Golden Globe awards, one for Best Motion Picture, Drama, and another for Best Screenplay.

Off-screen Emma also enjoyed another more personal reward from the film when she fell in love with co-star Greg Wise, cast as the nobleman. The two now have a daughter, who Thompson has referred to jokingly as 'jane.com', and were finally married in 2003.

The critics seem to agree that in spite of Laurie's few lines and limited time on-screen, he made a big impression. His reviews for this film were some of the best of his career up until that point, with even the US critics taking notice. *Variety* wrote, 'Hugh Laurie gets astonishing comic mileage out of a very small role as a chatterbox's husband.'

Films in Review said, 'Hugh Laurie as Staunton's acerbic husband, who has limited screen time, with minimal dialogue, is worth his weight in box office receipts. The man can do more with a raised eyebrow than most actors can with a long soliloquy.'

Not bad for a part which Hugh himself described as a role that called for 'about six lines'. The film brought him more recognition in the UK but, just as importantly, started to get him noticed on the other side of the Atlantic.

'My parents would constantly tell me how lucky I was. And that's where the guilt comes in. Well, am I worthy of this luck? Can I ever just rejoice in the fruits of my labours without this nagging voice of doubt in the back of my head?'

Hugh Laurie

CHAPTER 8

'I PLAY THE BADDIE.
IT'S A GOOD THING...'

Attempting to recreate a classic movie is a tall task. It's even tougher if that classic movie is one of Disney's best loved animated films. Nevertheless, in 1996, Walt Disney decided to do it all again, but this time with real actors – and dogs. *101 Dalmatians* was to be a live-action version written and directed by John Hughes who had scripted some of the most-successful films of the 1980s, such as *Home Alone* and *The Breakfast Club*.

Glenn Close starred as Cruella De Vil, Joely Richardson and Jeff Daniels as Anita and Roger, and Mark Williams as one of Cruella's henchman, Horace. And of course there was a lively cast of around 217 real Dalmatians, which were rounded up to play Pongo, Perdita and the other 99 Puppies.

Hugh took on the role of Jasper, the tall, skinny henchman of Cruella De Vil in the remake of the fabulous animated classic. It was a performance that was uncannily similar to the late, great Oliver Reed who starred as Bill Sykes in the movie, *Oliver Twist*, but a nicer version with a lot more humour and farce. Both he and Mark Williams, who hadn't worked together before, gelled on-screen as the incompetent thugs who continually botch up the crime and suffer abuse at the hands of their evil boss.

'I play the baddie. It's a good thing,' muttered Laurie. 'Children love baddies, which is a worrying thing, that they do love them. My daughter, who is two and a half, had an absolute obsession with Cruella De Vil. It's really alarming. We have to read about Cruella every single night and my daughter goes, "Naughty woman", but she loves it. I'm afraid that at the age of four or five she's going to dye her hair black or white.'

Hugh's children couldn't wait for the release of the film to see their father star in one of their favourite stories. They had seen the original cartoon version time after time after time and to them it was a dream come true. Getting to visit the set and the 200 puppies made it all the better.

The live version doesn't stray far from the original, with Roger, played by Jeff Daniels, an American video-game designer living in London and working on ideas for new games. He is also the owner of Pongo, the large male Dalmatian. Joely Richardson plays Anita, a British fashion designer who works for the House of De Vil and owns Perdita, the gentle female Dalmatian. The dog's puppies are of course stolen by Anita's boss, Cruella De Vil, who wants to make a Dalmatian coat out of their skins. Recruiting the help of all the other dogs in London, Pongo and Perdita set out to find and rescue all 99 pups from their fearsome captors, Jasper and

Horace (Laurie and Williams, respectively). Predictably, it all turns out well in the end as the Dalmatians are found and Roger designs a successful video game featuring Dalmatian puppies as the protagonists and Cruella as the villain.

Like most people who watched the non-animated version, Hugh was extremely impressed at how well Glenn Close excelled as the cartoon-like, fur-loving, family-hating fiend with a nasty streak of evilness running through every vein in her body. The blonde star individually made the infamous black-and-white haired creation into a new modern-day hate figure with kids and adults the world over.

Initially, Close rejected the role of Cruella due to scheduling conflicts with the stage musical *Sunset Boulevard* in which she was starring. Sigourney Weaver was then offered the role by the producers, but she too found herself in a similar predicament and also turned it down. Luckily, by that time casting was almost at a close, Close ended her run on Broadway, and at the second offer jumped at the chance.

'It was simply a character I couldn't resist. She is quite different from anything I've played before,' said the woman who had once boiled a bunny. 'I don't really think there is such a thing as going too far with her. She is the devil personified. She's almost not human. I went back to the animated film and stole things. Since Disney owns it, they told me I could use anything I wanted.'

To get into shape to play Cruella De Vil and to fit into the glamorous slinky costumes created by Academy Award-winning designer Anthony Powell, Close went on an extensive diet and trained hard everyday. 'She looked six feet tall and very bony in the cartoon film,' she said. 'I was determined to get that look but I almost crippled myself wearing those four-and-a-half inch heels. I had to learn to breathe with the corset, too. I almost fainted once. And the wig was disgusting. They put an egg in it to make the hair look sticky and they'd keep the wig in a refrigerator overnight.'

Even though on-screen she played an animal-hating monster, away from the cameras, Oscar-winning Glenn was actually completely the opposite. Furthermore, she insisted on wearing only fake fur during filming at the Shepperton Studios in west London, and apparently threw an almighty fit when she discovered the producers wanted to use real animal skins for one of her costumes.

The use of animal skins wasn't the only point of contention. One magazine aimed at dog breeders informed their readers not to see the film. They feared it would encourage people to run out and buy Dalmatian puppies and then abandon them as they grew into dogs. A leading dog breeder said 'It has taken 20 years for the breed to recover from the cartoon film. At that time large numbers of unsuitable people rushed out to buy dogs and then discarded them when their children grew bored.' But as they say, all publicity is good publicity.

Predictably, getting the pack of untrained animals to take directions on set turned out to be a nightmare. For once the phrase 'One shouldn't work with children and animals' wasn't to be underestimated. The Dalmatian breed is tremendously lively, requires a lot of attention, and is very difficult to keep as a pet. It took a major effort and lots of training, and trainers, to get the large batch of eight-week-old puppies to sit still for many scenes. It nearly drove the director around the bend. To help, the dog owners were also on hand to urge the pups to stay put!

Jeff Daniels said that on more than one occasion he immediately plopped himself into a chair in reaction to all the 'Sit!' commands being shouted out by the owners, only to be told by the director, 'Not you, Jeff.' But the pups knew exactly who was boss. On more than one occasion when Glenn appeared on the set as Cruella in full fright wig, make-up, and costume, the dogs would instantly settle down, and the dog playing Purdy repeatedly tried to slink away and hide under the table.

For some of the scenes, they got the dogs to lick the actors on cue by daubing steak juice on their skin. In one scene they actually rubbed raw hot dogs on Jeff Daniel's face to get the pups to appear friendly.

101 Dalmatians premiered in November of 1996 and set a Thanksgiving weekend record in the US, opening with $45 million dollars at the box office. It went on to perform very well, earning well over $300 million worldwide.

With the success of *101 Dalmatians*, Hugh continued to look for more opportunities on the big screen despite the feeling he was fighting a losing battle against all the snobbery that existed in the British film industry.

'There is among the British acting fraternity – which it isn't, by the way, it's a backstabbing snake pit – but let's pretend it's a fraternity. There is a snobbery about the movies that they're kind of commercial and the particularly American movies are more so.'

Still, the pretentiousness didn't stop him, and with a Disney classic under his belt, he moved on in search of little people who lived under the floorboards. During the Christmas season of 1997, *The Borrowers* saw Hugh starring alongside a fine troupe of actors from both sides of the Atlantic. The larger-than-life John Goodman enjoyed himself as the overstated Potter who doesn't have a kind bone in his body; Jim Broadbent is as impressive as usual as Pod, the father of the borrowers; and Celia Imrie and novice Flora Newbigin also starred. Again, as in *101 Dalmatians*, Mark Williams played a henchman, Jeff the 'Pest Control Operative', while this time Laurie did a full 180-degree turn and went from villain to an ultra-helpful village constable, Officer Steady.

The film, based on the 1952 children's book by Mary Norton, is still an all-time children's favourite and has been a successful stage play. It's about a family of thumb-sized little people called 'borrowers' who do exactly that as they scurry about in the homes of humans, borrowing their possessions and turning them into tiny pieces of furniture and other household necessities.

One of the main stars of the movie, John Goodman, told the *Irish News* that it was the chance to work with Hugh that was the 'real joy' of making *The Borrowers*. 'The first time I was over here was seven years ago, for a film called *King Ralph* with Peter O'Toole. Around that time, the first of the *Jeeves and Wooster* series came on. I've always been a Wodehouse fan and Stephen Fry and Hugh just knocked me out. I've been a fan ever since.'

Goodman and Laurie got along so well they actually hung out together off-set, enjoying a few beers together on more than one occasion.

Bringing the images created by Norton to life as a believable comedic fantasy-adventure was not easy. It could easily have failed without director Peter Hewitt, who had earlier directed *Bill & Ted's Bogus Journey* in 1991. He presented the story from two alternate perspectives, that of the normal-sized humans and that of the four-inch-high Borrowers. The producer, who was a devil for detail, left nothing for granted and took every precaution to ensure everything was perfect, from the enlarged objects used to highlight the small world of the borrowers to the massively impressive 1950s American gothic metropolis city where all the action takes place.

Although his role was small, Hugh's performance ensured he shared in the favourable comments from various critics, with many stating that along with Ruby Wax, his cameo appearance was top rate and superb as the interfering policeman.

The Borrowers turned out to be a funny and charming movie which appealed to adults as well as children. It was warmly received in Britain and labelled as 'the must-see family film of the Christmas season'. It received very good reviews in the US too. The following year it was nominated for the title of Best British Film in the British Academy of Film and Television Arts (BAFTA) awards but narrowly lost out to Gary Oldman's film, *Nil by Mouth*.

Playing a copper chasing little people around a house may have seemed a bit far fetched until Hugh appeared in a movie which many still believe is one of his most bizarre choices of roles thus far. In 1997, along with a bunch of other famous British actors, Laurie played a role, although fairly small, in helping the Spice Girls continue their world dominance with their film *Spice World*. A British musical comedy directed by Bob Spiers, it is similar in style to The Beatles' first movie, *A*

Hard Day's Night, which portrays the fictional events leading up to a major concert at London's Royal Albert Hall.

Director Spiers had been working in America on the Disney film *That Darn Cat* at the peak of the Spice Girls' popularity. When initially approached to direct the movie, Spiers claimed to have had no idea who the group was until his friend Jennifer Saunders encouraged him to give it some consideration.

Hugh plays Poirot, a role that is probably best forgotten by all involved, and one suspects probably doesn't appear on the front page of his acting CV. But he wasn't alone. Many other cameo stars popped up to make appearances throughout the film, such as Roger Moore, Elton John, Jennifer Saunders, Richard E. Grant, Michael Barrymore, Elvis Costello, old partner Stephen Fry and Meat Loaf, which thankfully kept it from completely wrecking his street credibility.

Other celebrities were pencilled in for various roles but for one reason or another didn't make the final cut. Ex-world heavyweight boxing champion Frank Bruno, playing the tour bus driver, left the film due to a personal disagreement with the Spice Girls and soon after went on to have a very public breakdown. He was replaced by Meat Loaf. Then there was shamed pop star Gary Glitter who did a four-minute cameo appearance as himself but shortly before the film was to be released he was arrested on child porn offenses. The Spice Girls and the production team agreed that his cameo should be deleted from the final print. They did however keep the scene of the girls performing the Gary Glitter song 'Leader of the Gang'.

On top of all that, the sudden death of two very public

figures not long after filming was completed prompted edits to be made quickly to the movie; mentions of Princess Diana and scenes including the designer Gianni Versace were cut out after their untimely deaths.

The film premiered on 15 December 1997 and was released in British cinemas on Boxing Day 1997, followed by its release in America in January 1998. It took $75 million dollars at the box office worldwide, but despite being a commercial success, the film was predictably widely panned by critics. The Spice Girls won the award for Worst Actress at the 1998 Golden Raspberries and the movie was mentioned in the 100 Most Enjoyably Bad Movies Ever Made list.

Hugh put it all down to experience and after a series of cameo performances found himself in a major role in the film adaptation of the Honoré de Balzac novel *Cousin Bette*. His co-stars included Jessica Lange, Elizabeth Shue, Kelly Macdonald, Bob Hoskins and Aden Young. Hugh played Baron Hulot, widower brother-in-law of Jessica Lange, in a tale of betrayal and revenge in mid-19th-century Paris. The film opened in North America in June 1998, and premiered in the UK at the Edinburgh Festival in the August.

The film received good reviews and so did the rising ex-Footlights star. 'Like a perfect martini, Hugh concocts the right mixture of humour, vanity, and self-pity. This weak-willed gent ruins his family for the love of a skirt without a single moment of insight or regret, and remains likeable. That's the brilliance and folly of Balzac's human comedy!' said the *New York Post* in June 1998.

On the same day the *Chicago Tribune* printed: 'The rest of the cast is also strong, especially Hugh Laurie as the vain and preoccupied Hector, and Kelly Macdonald (*Trainspotting*) as the scheming and morally bankrupt Hortense.'

As the year 2000 got closer, Hugh appeared on a few well-known TV sitcoms, the most famous of which was a walk-on part in the US hit show *Friends* in 1998, where he played a gentleman on a plane.

He felt so privileged to be asked to appear in such a top-quality American show because unlike many more vocal British stars, he is actually a fan of everything American. 'Part of the reason is that television had a factory feel,' he admitted. 'It is perceived as a craft, rather than an art. But I think a good episode of *ER* is as good as drama gets. Good TV can be astonishing. I just adore them as works of absolute genius. There is an attitude here [in the UK] which I find rather offensive, of condescending to American TV.'

After *Friends*, Hugh guest-starred in a few episodes of the British spy series *Spooks*, a show he was also a big fan of, because of his fascination with espionage and everything to do with the world of spies.

It was also a busy time for his vocal cords as his prominent voice was again very much in demand in a variety of shows and films in the 90s. He began as Squire Trelawney in eight episodes of *The Legends of Treasure Island* in 1993. It was followed by Johnny Town-Mouse in *The World of Peter Rabbit and Friends* two years later; in the same year, there was *The Snow Queen's Revenge*. Then in 1997 *The Ugly Duckling* and Mr Wolf in the cartoon *Preston Pig*. There were many others, right up to the British film *Valiant*, but one of the most interesting was in 2001 when he voiced the character of a bar patron in the cult

US TV series *Family Guy*, in an episode entitled 'One If by Clam. Two If by Sea'.

He has also appeared in a few pop videos, following up his appearance in Kate Bush's video for 'Experiment IV' with a hilarious cameo as Prince George in full Regency-period costume, and in Annie Lennox's song 'Walking on Broken Glass' in 1992 opposite John Malkovich, who also appeared in character as Vicomte de Valmont from *Dangerous Liaisons*.

The world of TV, films and the fame that goes with it was slowly becoming a way of life, whether Hugh liked it or not.

'The money is better in films but *101 Dalmatians* seemed to take 101 years to make. Film can be a lot better than television, but it can also be a lot worse. Some of the best things you see these days are TV shows, but films seem to have more glamour. Brad Pitt is more glamorous than, let's say, Ellen DeGeneres.'

Hugh Laurie

CHAPTER 9

'IT'S FOUR WEDDINGS
AND A FUNERAL WITH
BALLS AND A ****'

'Hugh is so sexy,' Ben Elton commented. 'I always knew there was a romantic lead deep inside him. He has deep blue eyes, he's muscular. I've got him playing piano in a T-shirt with those big biceps bulging.'

All those who had watched Laurie growing up in the public eye knew he was an extremely funny man as well as a talented musician, and they may even have known he was a devoted family man, but few would have put him down as a romantic lead or a sex symbol, a label that embarrassed Hugh immensely. But that was all about to change.

When Elton's book *Inconceivable* hit the bestseller list, it didn't take long before there was talk of turning it into a movie. A slightly less obvious decision was the fact that the writer, who also directed the film, would ask one of his best friends, a man normally linked with slapstick comedy, to take on the role as the romantic lead in the movie. The screen film, entitled *Maybe Baby*, featured Joely Richardson, who had also appeared with him in *101 Dalmatians*, as his wife Lucy. In the movie, Hugh and Joely play a healthy, good-looking married couple, both with very successful careers but without the one thing they want most of all: a baby.

Ben, who had known Laurie for 20 years, was quite vocal as to why he had gone against the grain and the powers that be to cast Laurie in the star role of the film.

'The secret is out. Hugh's a great actor. I always felt with him that there was a secret waiting to be let out. He thinks a great deal. He is not good at selling himself. Of course he's terrific at comedy, playing the amiables and the idiots, but those who know him well, and not that many do, know that as well as doubt and insecurity he has great inner strength; huge depth and thoughtfulness. When I asked him to play Sam, he was all, "Blimey, Ben! Do you think I can do it?" But when I looked at him through the camera, the vulnerability was heartbreaking. He is a complicated fellow, and really quite special.' The writer added without a hint of jest, 'He's our new Cary Grant or Tom Hanks. He looks fantastic. He and Joely are an exquisite couple. I think they're Britain's answer to Tom Hanks and Meg Ryan,' says Elton.

Joely Richardson was more than willing to agree with Ben. 'Hugh is mysterious, and very beautiful. I met him during *101 Dalmatians*. I was sort of fascinated by him. I found him mysterious. There is a lot more to him than comedy, though he is brilliant at that; he has comic timing no amount of money can buy.'

Naturally, Hugh, a little more down-to-earth, commented, 'It's plainly very flattering he thinks of me in those terms. I don't know what to say. Maybe he sent the script to Tom Hanks, who turned it down, and then Ben willed himself to think of me as Tom. Maybe, if he'd got Christopher Biggins for the part he'd have said the same about him.'

It was the typical witty response one would expect from the star. Yet, deep down, being asked by Ben to play the main role had genuinely taken him aback. 'Deeply flattered to get the chance to play a romantic lead, never done before, and flattered because Ben had written the script which was largely about his own life. Although he will say it's not autobiographical, it's very much drawn on his own experience. So he sort of comes to me and says, "Will you play me in a film?" That's quite an honour, to have your best friend say he wants you to play him.' He also quickly added that of course his mate Ben was 'completely insane.'

Although Ben's wife, Sophie Gare, became pregnant after Elton finished writing *Inconceivable*, the similarities between real life and his humorous storyline were obvious. In the story, the married couple, Sam and Lucy, try everything humanly possible to conceive including some bizarre New Age chanting, acupuncture and other peculiar methods until they embark on a course of IVF treatments in an attempt to have a baby. Sam, who works in TV comedy, decides to use their dilemma along with his psoriasis problem as the storyline for a movie script he is hoping will get him out of his tedious day job. A situation very similar to what Ben and Sophie had actually experienced, including the psoriasis.

Elton was quoted as saying that out of all the books he has written, this is definitely the most personal book so far, although he is at pains to point out that it is fiction. 'My wife and I have been through IVF and I know a lot about it, but Sam and Lucy are not Ben and Sophie. For a start, I'm more relaxed than Sam, and he's more of a twit than me. It is about what can happen when you want something so much you risk losing what you already have.'

During the series of IVF treatments in London, Ben admitted he often felt like a 'freak', a 'sad act sitting there with a load of other sad acts'. Their relationship was put under considerable strain by the process of trying to conceive. After their second IVF failure, he privately resigned himself to the fact that they would never have a baby. Their setbacks were sad and upsetting and Ben said they coped by 'getting drunk and smoking 20 fags'.

But it became third time lucky when Sophie became pregnant. Even though the twins were born nine weeks premature and weighed in at only four pounds each, it was the cause of much rejoicing. 'It was a monumental step for us, enough to celebrate big time,' said Ben after they had twins. 'Then, out of the blue there is a even bigger love happening, double trouble, two babies, instant family.' Typically, like most men, he insisted the whole process was much tougher for his wife and mentioned that when the twins were born, he didn't experience the blinding emotional high he expected, but laughed because they looked so funny. While his wife fell instantly in love with her new babies, Elton's reaction was more complex. 'Look, I'm won't pretend I went "Aaaaaahh!" when I first saw them. I love them deeply and I will do anything for their happiness and wellbeing, but there has been no drama- scene moment for me.' His children were hooked up on tubes and drips for the first weeks; little Bert even had a drip needle going into his head, protected by a plastic cup. Nonetheless, it turned out to be a happy ending for the writer and his wife.

Maybe Baby provided the second opportunity for Hugh and Joely Richardson to work together and he was more than delighted to have another chance. 'I was thrilled when she agreed to do the part, mainly because she's a proper actress. It was exciting for me because I was feeling not like a proper actor and I wanted a bit of properness going on, and so did Ben because it was his first time directing a film.' He added, 'She's beautiful, very bright, funny and she has such command, or is the word poise, terrific poise, and on top of all that she has this terrific vulnerability.'

Joely was just as complimentary about the man she called special. 'Hugh has this heartbreaking quality. When his face is still, the pathos is extraordinary. There are two sides to him. There's the Hugh who dances around and cracks jokes, tangos all over the place. And there's the other side: tortured, dark. I love them both.'

It was Elton's knack of getting the right balance between comedy and drama which proved people, who didn't think Laurie was up to the mark, completely wrong. He stepped quite naturally into the leading man role without the need to hide behind the face gestures and slapstick humour, alongside Richardson who also excelled in her role as the young woman whose life is slowly falling to pieces because the one thing she desired most in the world is just beyond her grasp.

But his performance wasn't without its moments of anxiety. The emotional scenes in which he had to show grief caused Hugh a bit of his own personal grief. It physically shook him up. 'I felt as if I'd had a near-miss in a car crash. I was physically shaking. Thing is, I've never trained as an actor. I've got no diploma in acting out grief. I don't know the "normal" way to do it.' There was honesty in his admission and the struggle he faced was evident. 'Is the object to care utterly or not to care at all? Should I access grief, as they put it, and trust the camera will see that, so if I'm feeling something truthful, that will emerge? Or am I going for the lightness of grief? Do I just have to resemble grief, represent it, and not let myself be filled with it? It's like that famous example in *Marathon Man*, with Laurence Olivier saying to Dustin Hoffman, "You should try acting, dear boy, it's an awful lot easier."' Hugh still isn't sure how he came through it all unscathed. 'The truth is, I don't know. I don't know what I would do again if I had to. I've not trained in this job, acting. I don't feel like an actor. What does an actor feel like? Not like me, anyway.'

However it wasn't only letting the grief pour out of him, which caused him sleepless nights. He discovered the first day on the set that he had to act out one of his worst nightmares, a scene in which he and Joely spend the whole day performing an energetic love scene. In the story he is required to have sex whenever his wife decrees that the time is right. When his character, an executive with BBC television, gets the call, he jumps on his motorcycle and roars off home, ripping off his clothes as soon as he gets to the front door.

'I was only allowed to wear a sock,' he says. 'But the only way to do the shot was to be naked. It's been my worst nightmare ever since the showers at school. I couldn't believe I was living it. He admitted that the night before they started shooting, he didn't sleep a wink and all the stress nearly sent him over the edge.

There was a fair amount of hanky-panky required and Laurie admits, 'I'd never done anything resembling a bed scene in my life before. I was losing my film virginity, as it were, and that was a very strange experience. It felt hysterical when we were doing it, but some bits were very difficult, having to let go when the camera's rolling. Being English, it's hard to let go and to trust that it's going to be all right. It's scary.' The fear, or maybe relief, was evident in his eyes as he continued. 'It wasn't a case of the sex scenes being very heavy. It was just the fact I was there naked in front of an entire crew. Ben had asked me to work out before we started shooting so I did three sit-ups every morning to get ready for that dreaded moment. Fortunately the shots involved a lot of humour, so hopefully the attention is not entirely on my body. It was scary, thinking, "Today, not only have I got to act, but I've got to do it in a romantic leading man kind of way." But Joely is a lot more experienced at making films and doing romantic scenes, so in a lot of ways she set the tone by being very supportive, and tried to relax me, but I said, "Look, I've only just got used to doing this kind of thing in front of one person."'

Taking his trousers off and exposing himself in front of an entire film crew, the actor says, is probably the bravest thing the boy raised a Presbyterian had ever done. He doesn't even like watching other people's sex scenes in films and can't stand to see other people kissing in public. 'I feel voyeuristic. It's crazy. I know. I would look away, and I want to do the same when I see it on film.'

In real life he reckons the act of sex itself is traumatic enough and an awkward business on the best of times. 'After all, it's not something other people do in front of you in real life. We might watch people having an argument or running down a street. But if they started taking their clothes off and having sex in front of you, I'm out of the door pretty sharpish. It happened to me once when I was sharing a tent with Dutch hippies in Morocco. It wasn't an issue for them, but it was for me. So I went for an incredibly long walk. Even then, it wasn't long enough as it turns out because I arrived back in time for the second bout. And I had walked an awful long way.'

He added, 'If there is only two of you in the room, not embarrassing, but it's not a moment, well not something you slip into casually, when you've got 50 well-fed men in jeans standing about looking at you, 50 men with opinions of what you should be doing and how you should be doing it. What I notice is you start to develop the most amazing peripheral vision. You start to see people out of the corner of your eye while you are about to kiss, hear them saying things like, "Is that how he's going to do it?"'

Hugh felt as though he was being judged on his performance. 'It's a bit scary. But now I consider myself qualified. Oh shit, I don't know if they should issue a little diploma saying, "Has performed first sex scene" on it.'

The rocky road that his personal life had taken also made the on-screen love-making more tricky. It had started before *Maybe Baby* when he was away in South Africa filming a children's movie, *The Place of Lions*. While there, he became involved with the director, Audrey Cooke. Hugh has always kept his private life out of the public eye but when people started to gossip, Hugh dashed back to England to tell his wife of 11 years what had happened. Before *Maybe Baby*, they patched things up and Hugh said their relationship was back on track and he was 'very much' back at home with Jo and their children. 'Nothing I can say will make it any better, so it's best I say nothing,' he said. 'Everything is back on track at home.' And it was during Ben's movie that he did confirm that they intended to stay together. It was rumoured that friends of the couple said the experience left Cooke devastated, and Jo was so defiant and determined to save her marriage that she wrote an emotional letter to Cooke, begging her to stop seeing her husband.

It was of course an episode that he wasn't particularly proud of in his life, an episode he needed to face up to. 'It would be awful for me to sit here saying, "Poor me. Life is so hard. Everywhere there is temptation." You just have to deal with what you are dealt. I don't know if it's any more difficult for an actor than a travelling salesman. And I quibble with the word glamour. It would be very odd if you saw your own life as glamorous. How would you order a hamburger, for instance, in a glamorous way?'

With his wife's forgiveness, the family had no problems watching his love scenes with Joely in the new film.

'My wife read the script and there was no mention made. And one time I had to kiss Joely and one of my sons was watching and he just looked appalled, which is great. I'm now at the stage where I can embarrass him.'

Despite his fears on and off screen, Hugh got through the experience with flying colours and he thanked Ben for working extremely hard to create a terrific atmosphere where everyone felt confident that they weren't going to be made a fool of. 'It was very light-touch. I've got nothing to compare it with, I've never done something like this before, it was a real departure for me.'

Even with the lack of confidence in himself and the embarrassing scenes, Hugh enjoyed the role immensely and even took over the reigns of director when Elton went to the hospital for the birth of his children. But however much he enjoyed the extra responsibly, he did find it 'almost unbearable' to watch himself when the scenes were being played back on the monitor. He would stand there, head in hands, wanting nothing more than to quickly walk away. Seeing himself act is something Hugh just can't get his head around. If the truth is known, he never or rarely ever watches himself in a film or on TV.

'I stopped watching myself a long time ago because I find it very painful. I'm constantly thinking, "Oh, if only I'd done this or why did I do it like that?" You know, you have good days and bad days.'

He never reads articles about himself either, even if they are good, and feels the same about giving interviews. 'Obviously you are in a very vulnerable position when you give an interview. You are putting your testicles on a chopping board,' he muttered. 'Interviews steal your soul, your identity, your privacy.'

Most people, unless they are very big headed, dislike hearing their own voices or seeing themselves on screen; Hugh is no different. 'Most of us wince at how far short we fall from the picture we have of ourselves. It's hard to watch yourself, but worse than watching yourself, is listening to yourself.

When you hear your own voice inside your head, your voice is interesting; it goes up and down and is full of light and shade and emotion. When you hear it, though, it's horrible.'

He even found watching the first viewing with some friendly faces to be a murderous ordeal. He watched it with his fingers in his cars. 'I pushed them so far in I thought they were going to start bleeding. Then we watched it with a bigger audience and it was a relief because it got some big laughs.'

Maybe Baby was warmly received, with many critics unanimous in their opinion that the supporting cast were the ones that really stole the show. Due to Elton being Elton, he had amassed a talented array of actors to play small cameo roles. Emma Thompson turned up as a bizarre New Age guru. Dawn French is hilarious as an over-the-top Australian IVF nurse, Joanna Lumley from *Absolutely Fabulous* is the hellish tough lesbian manager of a theatrical agency, the uniquely talented Rowan Atkinson plays a slightly strange obstetrician, and Tom Hollander plays the Scottish film director.

'Dawn French was absolutely brilliant,' Hugh commented, 'She was only there for about two days to do it and it's very annoying when you are there for months working on this and someone comes in and steals the whole blasted thing in two days. She goes driving off saying bye and everyone says, "Oh wasn't she great."'

On Rowan, with whom he had of course worked in the *Blackadder* series, Hugh just shook his head and muttered, 'I just watched him and marvelled. He's a different kind of animal, he's self contained. He has a different way of going about his job. And he's very concentrated, very focused. He thinks about everything, every mille-second of what's he going to do. Take after take you find yourself finding some extra little bits. It was joyous to watch. He's magnificent.'

As with the cast, the sound track is also full of top talent including Paul McCartney singing the title track written by Buddy Holly, 'Maybe Baby', plus many others including Westlife, Roxy Music, Lene Marlin, Atomic Kitten, Elvis Costello & the Attractions, George Michael and Madness.

Even though Hugh felt unworthy, he also felt extremely lucky to be given the opportunity. He knew it was a risk for him and Ben, but in the end it was a risk absolutely worth taking, for both of them. 'Being asked to be the romantic lead was a very frightening thing. To actually shoulder the whole thing and become this George Clooney-ish kind of guy was very daunting. Thankfully Ben took a gamble on me and I hope I've repaid his faith with a decent performance.'

'He is actually one of the most down-to-earth people in show business and we became mates very quickly. I don't think he's changed much at all over the past 20 years, but he will change in the public perception after this film.'

Ben Elton

CHAPTER 10

'HEIGHT JOKES WERE NOT WELL RECEIVED'

Who could have imagined for one minute that after working long and hard on British TV, not to mention the big screen, that playing the loving father of an adopted animated mouse would turn out to be one of Hugh's most commercially successful gigs?

Laurie's bank manager probably didn't see it coming, but he or she must have been over the moon as the phenomenon known as *Stuart Little* took the world by storm and beyond.

The first movie in the series, released in 1999, was very loosely based on the novel by children's author E.B. White, who also wrote *Charlotte's Web*. It is about a mouse that is adopted by the Little family and the adventures that he encounters as he tries to become an accepted member of the family. The idea for the novel, published in 1945, came to life when White fell asleep on a train but the story ends rather abruptly because White, a bit of a hypochondriac, thought he was going to die soon, so he ended the book rather quickly in order to get it published before his death. White in fact lived another 40 years after the book's publication. Lucky for Hugh, Walt Disney's inspiration to make *Stuart Little* into an animated classic in 1954 fell through and it stayed in book format until Sony Pictures picked up the option in 1999.

The film combined live action, including real animals, with computer animation, but the storyline bore little resemblance to that of the original book. In fact, only some of the characters and one or two minor plot elements are the same.

When initially offered the role, Hugh thought it was a story about some kind of rat creature. Then an American friend explained how popular the book was and after a second reading of the script, he decided it was the perfect book for his children to read. 'I find it's a struggle to get children to read anything and to get them away from the PlayStation and Pokémon, which is driving me up the wall. I don't understand what it is, but my kids can sit around discussing Pokémon and swapping cards for hours. All I got when I was a child was a yo-yo and a few toy soldiers.'

Stuart Little stars Geena Davis as Mrs Eleanor Little, the mother of Stuart and her human son, George. Hugh plays Mr Frederick Little, the father, while Jonathan Lipnicki, who was the little boy in the film *Jerry Maguire*, plays George Little, the brother of the adopted mouse.

The voice of Stuart Little himself was done to perfection by Michael J. Fox. Nathan Lane is the voice of Snowbell 'Snow', the Little's cynical house cat, and Chazz Palminteri voiced Smokey the Russian Blue alley cat, the powerful mafia-Don type who leads the alley cats. Smokey serves as the main antagonist and villain of the film along with Monty the Mouth, voiced by Steve Zahn, one of Snowbell's closest friends who wants to eat Stuart.

'Making a children's film is harder than people think. People think you just take an adult film and make it slightly less well,' Laurie commented. 'That's a patronising assumption, but in fact, it's not true. It's very difficult to make one well, make it satisfying and commercially successful.'

His audition for the film was not exactly what you would call normal, but doing abnormal interviews and auditions had become a part of life for the star. 'With *101 Dalmatians* it was a case of auditioning like everyone else. I had to work really hard for it. This one they just asked me. I had to audition to Rob Minkoff [the director] for the role of Mr Little, over a mobile phone, standing on the street in London. I'd gone out for dinner and suddenly he called up and said, "I'm considering you, but I'm concerned about the American accent and how it will sound." I think he faxed a page of dialogue to the restaurant, and I was standing under a streetlight trying to see it. I know it sounds kind of ramshackle, doesn't it, for a $150 million movie, but that was the way it happened.'

Minkoff, the co-director of the Oscar-winning *The Lion King*, remembers the audition with Laurie, pretending to be an American over the phone, well. 'Hugh provided a first-rate impression, though he was, of course, rather critical of himself. Once he landed the role, he worked with a dialect coach every day to perfect his inflection and intonation.' Minkoff added, 'Hugh is very smart and never accepts things at face value. Every word of the script is analysed for its meaning, and every movement for its expressiveness.' After getting to know the British actor better, Rob described Hugh as 'the epitome of perfectionism' and praised the way he could capture a scene perfectly with just 'a goofy line or a look'.

As well as making a significant amount of money, *Stuart Little* proved to be the film that introduced Hugh to a worldwide audience, especially in the States. With the hype around it so massive, shops ran out of *Stuart Little* merchandise in the approach to Christmas. Hugh was again perplexed as to how he wound up in *Stuart Little* in the first place. 'It was probably a typing error. It's not as if I'm really known over there. *Blackadder*'s popular on cable, but I was only in 12 of those. And there's the P.G. Wodehouse I guess. But basically I'm not known at all. I don't even know what they were looking for. Was it "Find me some English guy" or "Let's have this guy, oh he's English is he?"' To this day he still questions why they hired an English actor to play an American, especially with all the other great actors waiting in the wings. 'They probably just wanted someone tall to play opposite Geena Davis. Most Americans aren't tall. They've got big heads but tiny bodies. Like tadpoles,' he joked. 'An awful lot of big Hollywood actors are about that size [he squeezed an inch between his thumb and forefinger]. It's cheaper because, if they're that size, the sets can be smaller. I'm 6ft 2 or something. I can't think of any qualifications at all. I can only see a clerical error that they went with.'

Even up to the point he arrived at the airport to start filming, he still thought someone was going to say, 'Oh, my God, it's the wrong guy! We thought it was the other guy.'

Nonetheless, being relatively unknown in the States meant

that there were no expectations for Hugh to be the same Hugh Laurie as he was in Great Britain. 'Absolutely none. You are more free to be whatever the part demands in the US. In fact, because I was worried about the accent, I decided it would be easier to be American the whole time rather than to try and go in and out of it. Also, Americans have no tolerance for foreign accents. They just don't understand what you're saying. So, if you're going to buy milk or a newspaper, it's easier to be American than go through the, "You what, you what, you wanna what?" routine. So most people didn't even know I was English. Or that's what I like to think.'

Like everything else in 'the bigger the better' America, the sheer size of the project amazed him. It felt wonderful to go to a big American studio and swank about as if he was the new Clark Gable (or if he had listened to Ben Elton, the new Cary Grant). 'It was a fantasy really, terrific fun and Hollywood was exactly as it says it would be on the tin. Hollywood has better weather, better lunches, bigger trailers and ten times more money. I enjoyed it all immensely. For the first *Stuart Little*, the Central Park set was about the same size as the real Central Park. Had that been done in Britain, it would've been one lamppost and a bin liner, and maybe a man with a dog walking through but that would have met the budget of £150.'

What he also liked about America was that he could walk around and not get recognised. 'I'm completely anonymous here,' he smirks. 'Not that life is unbearable in Britain. In fact, the really nice thing about my career is that the only people who do recognise me are those who actually like me, which is a good thing. I know some very famous people in England and they have a horrible time when they're recognised. I was out with Kenneth Branagh one night and it was incredible, drunk people feel they can say anything. One guy shouted over to him, "Branagh you're a c**t" and walked away.'

The closest he got to being recognised was being mistaken for actor Kevin Kline. 'People are very odd. I know this is about to occur when they start to behave like you're Kevin Kline. This awful feeling usually comes over me and I decide to go with it. I start saying "*A Fish Called Wanda* was a lot of fun to do..." but it makes them happy. Anyway, if I pointed out they were wrong, they'd feel silly, so it's better to just go with it and then they tell their friends, "I met Kevin Kline today."'

Obviously, the unusual storyline about a family adopting a talking mouse is risky, a risk which could have bombed. Even Hugh wasn't quite sure why the couple actually adopted the mouse. Months after the movie had finished, he was still in the dark, but he did add, 'Why adopted? It's even weirder in the book actually because Mrs Little gives birth to a mouse. Of course you try and do that on film and it's... tricky.'

Joking aside, the film called for some masterful special effects to make the fantasy romp come to life. In fact, it received an Academy Award nomination for Best Visual Effects, and took around two years after human filming had ceased before it was ready for release.

Jason Clark, co-producer of the film, reveals the simple truth of Stuart's birth which took three years to create. 'We couldn't find a trained mouse that could wear clothes, walk on two feet and deliver lines so we had to come up with a way to use technology to tell the story. What we did with Stuart Little wouldn't have been possible five years ago. The challenge was to use this futuristic digital wizardry to capture the spirit of a classic character that E.B. White created 50 years ago.'

The animators wanted to make Stuart as believable a character as possible so the audience would forget he was computer generated and think he was as real as the other actors. Rob Minkoff added, 'First you study mice and what they really look like and then you extract from that a kind of caricature which gives personality to the creation. We needed to find different ways of exaggerating what seems natural about a mouse, without falling into the trap of being too cute.'

They created the actions and movements of the mouse by copying mime artist Bill Irwin, who would look at the script and act out the scene. One of the biggest obstacles to overcome was bringing the mouse's eyes to life and showing the reflection of the world in his pupils. The animators got over it by photographing a silver ball that had a reflection of the set in it, which they put into Stuart's eye.

A lot of work and expense went into creating a series of model mice for the various scenes throughout the movie. The way they worked fascinated Hugh. 'We had some little robot ones that kind of moved about manically and had about 19 people with remote control things, but mostly it's...perhaps I shouldn't really be giving this away. I mean we all want to believe don't we? No, it was a computer that did it all so we were acting to nothing, which is strangely pleasurable, most of the time, a lot easier than real actors.' With the exception of the rest of the cast and Michael J. Fox, of course, who Laurie met and worked with for the first time.

'We rehearsed with Michael,' Laurie mentioned. 'He wasn't there when we were shooting because he's got this big sitcom,

Spin City, which he was off making. But we had some rehearsal with him. He's a very nice man, and very funny. He did it incredibly well.'

Hugh's character in the film, Mr Little, is a very good-hearted chap with bucketfuls of patience, which Hugh believes is not a trait that mirrors his own personality. 'I'm rather crotchety, to put it mildly, and something of a let-down to my own children, but I do my best, and they're very forgiving, thankfully.' In the world of parenthood he places himself more in the 'slightly used man' camp than in the 'new modern men' one. 'I try to get up in the night for the kids and do my bit, but I'm, well, Stephen has accused me of narcolepsy, of being able to fall asleep anywhere. If a taxi toots its horn five miles away, Jo is awake. Yet there have been mornings when she's put the children to bed next to me, and I haven't woken up. You could fire a shotgun and I wouldn't wake.'

As with *101 Dalmatians*, Hugh's children must have been more than happy the day he came home to tell them the news about his new role. 'They're a pretty tough crowd, my children. I suppose my main goal is not to embarrass them too much because they've got to go into the playground and look their classmates in the eye, and if they've got other children going "Your Dad's crap!" that would obviously be tough on them! So I hope I haven't embarrassed them too much.'

What was far from embarrassing for the kids was the luxury of flying to LA to visit their father on the *Stuart Little* set. 'There are perks. They came out to Los Angeles when we were shooting there, for a couple of weeks, and they came onto the set, which was good fun. They got some goodie bags. They got some baseball caps and T-shirts out of it.'

The hardest part of all for Hugh and the other members of the cast was to act as if Stuart was really there as they listened to Michael J. Fox deliver Stuart's lines. To make it easier, they would either look at a laser pointer or a ball dangling from a fishing pole to get the sight lines correct for the camera. Davies and Laurie spent lots of time acting to empty air and spaces which were filled in later by the animators and computer-generated imagery.

'It's hell, absolutely gruelling,' joked Laurie, swiftly adding, 'It isn't actually, at all. The trick is that all film-making is about imagining something that isn't there, that's almost always the way it happens. If you play a scene where you have to react to the *Titanic* going down, they don't sink the *Titanic* just so you can look at it, they do it with a tennis ball on a stick. We have one advantage over *Men in Black II* in that we know what a mouse looks like. In that film they've got to imagine sixty foot aliens with nine heads coming out of the subway, and that's nine tennis balls on sticks, so we had it easy.'

In one particularly emotional shot, Geena Davis gently hands Stuart to Hugh. 'She tips her hand down, and Stuart slides off,' explains visual effects supervisor Jerome Chen. 'The close-up of Stuart being transferred from one hand to another was very difficult, mainly because of the match move and shadowing that was required.'

The process began on set with Davis and Laurie practising the move by holding a puppet that provided a sense of weight. 'We had Geena cup her hand to give Stuart a place to sit,' says Chen. 'We also made sure that Hugh moved his hand to the right place.'

Geena Davis, who perversely felt she was just perfect for her role in *Stuart Little* due to her vast experience with interspecies relationships as the girlfriend of *The Fly*, and kissing aliens in *Earth Girls Are Easy*. She said playing opposite an empty space was tricky at first. 'We have to figure out where everyone is looking, and it takes a long time to get all this organised. If he's moving, they have a laser pointer so we can follow it, and the camera is timed so the pointer doesn't come on the film, so they have nothing to erase later.'

During one take, Hugh pretends to pick up Stuart and talk to him. When the director shouted 'Cut' Laurie actually placed the mouse, which obviously wasn't in his hands, down gently onto a table. 'I thought, "Hang on a minute, that's mad. The next time the director said cut, I thought, "No, I'm not putting him down" and so I just opened my hands. But then I automatically screamed out and looked at the floor to make sure he was OK and I hadn't broken his pelvis or something.'

It was all good fun on the set, where everyone got into the 'Stuart is real' fan club. During interviews, Hugh would comment on the little mouse's acting talent. 'There is something Brando-ish about him, but don't think that hasn't gone to his head. The first thing he said to me when I met him was, "Stay out of my light." He's just aware of his image, as all these big stars are.' Stuart even had a small trailer and a canvas chair with his name on it.

When asked if Stuart was sensitive about being three inches tall, Hugh added, 'Height jokes were not well received in the first week. He made it pretty clear that anything to do with cheese was not funny. We had a couple of good cheese jokes in the script, actually, but they had to go.'

Although Stuart was animated, the other animals in the movie were not. Boone's Animals for Hollywood trained 23 cats of various breeds to portray the eight cats in the film, and it took the same number of cat trainers hidden in various spots on the set to direct the cats in their performances.

On its opening weekend, *Stuart Little* grossed $15 million, placing it at Number 1. It went on to amass a worldwide total of over $300 million, not bad for such an unlikely story. It covered its budget and was a box office success. It was ranked as the second highest-grossing film of all time with a rat theme, behind *Ratatouille*.

It also received quite an unusual award from The National Fatherhood Initiative (NFI) in the 2000 Daddy Awards in the category of Best Portrayal of Fatherhood in an animated or family feature. Being honoured with the 2000 Daddy were Hugh Laurie and producer Douglas Wick. 'The Daddy Awards offer an opportunity to focus on the positive impact that the entertainment media can play in helping to promote responsible fatherhood,' said NFI president Wade F. Horn, Ph.D.

Of course no sooner had the film finished filming than there was already talk of a sequel to follow. Hugh wasn't sure what would happen; he hadn't been involved with a sequel to a movie before. 'As an actor you go where the wind takes you. It's very hard to be in films if you've not been asked, believe me I've tried. To be perfectly honest I thought my own part in this film was just being a pair of ankles really, just walking through the frame every now and then. Finely turned out ankles, I like to think, but ankles none the less! It's hard to say what's directly come of it. Certainly it's great to be involved with something as successful as this, and particularly in America.'

The film's massive success did increase his profile in Hollywood tenfold, and Laurie admired how there is a different mindset in Hollywood compared to the rest of the world as far as film-making is concerned. 'If you're an actor and you want to do films then, because it so happens that Americans control films worldwide, sooner or later you will have to take their filthy coin. Albeit a very large coin. Hollywood with all its absurdities, and it has plenty of those, Hollywood makes the best movies in the world. It just does. And it's pointless to try and pretend otherwise. We may try to reassure ourselves that Hollywood is Babylon and there are great works of art done elsewhere, and of course, every now and then, there will be a good English film, or good French film or good Romanian film or whatever.' He also said, 'But basically, in terms of just sheer numbers, Hollywood provides fantastic entertainment and terrific films. This isn't just me toadying to Hollywood because I'm here at the time. I've always thought that. The films I've loved ever since I was a kid, 90 per cent of them came from this town.'

As much as he liked and admired the States, at the time, Hugh said he had absolutely no intention of following the likes of many other British actors who settled in California. 'I've got three children and it would be a big wrench to say, "Come on, we're going to California, there's gold in them hills." Especially if there may not be and a year later we'd have to come back, stony broke.'

Of course he didn't have to worry about begging on the streets because with the success of the original *Stuart Little* film, the sequel wasn't far behind. In 2002, with a $100 million budget, the second movie was born. This time the storyline mirrored more closely the original novel, while maintaining the wittiness, appealing characters, great special effects and wholesome family values of the first one.

In *Stuart Little 2* everyone's favourite talking mouse gains a new friend in a bird called Margolo (voiced by Melanie Griffith) who he rescues from a villainous falcon, voiced by James Woods. Meanwhile, as well as trying to keep Stuart out of trouble, Mr and Mrs Little also have a new addition to the family, a daughter (a real one this time), Martha, played in turn by twins Anna and Ashley Hoelck.

'We have a daughter in this one,' said Hugh. 'We never really worked out in mouse years how old Stuart is, but he's on the cusp of adolescence, which implies all sorts of problems...no, not problems, opportunities. He finds love, then loses it, then finds it again.'

Geena Davis was actually pregnant during some of the re-shoots and several techniques were used to hide her pregnancy.

By this second instalment, Hugh had honed his American accent even further. He also voiced the same role for the animated series, also known simply as *Stuart Little*, for HBO in 2003. It was aired for just one season and contained 13 episodes. Then, finally, a third and final film, *Stuart Little 3: Call of the Wild* was released direct to video in 2006. It again featured Hugh as the father but had a different visual style, being entirely computer-animated. It wasn't the best, and on all accounts is best forgotten.

On reflection, the first two films were perfect for Laurie and came at just the right time. It got him in front of the American audiences in a big way and his fake, but very convincing, American accent opened a brand new world for him, one which would get much bigger a few years later.

'I still don't know why they chose me. I still think it was a typing error and they got the wrong bloke. They probably wanted Hugh Grant. The pleasurable thing about being in my position is that the only people who know who I am, like what I do. Tom Cruise is recognisable to a lot of people who hate Tom Cruise, and that's a horrible thing. It's strange, but many people who recognise me don't even know who I am.'

Hugh Laurie

CHAPTER 11

'I'M ON MY WAY
BACK TO MISERY'

'I was miserable, self-absorbed and selfish until I finally faced up to the truth of my depression.' It was around the time of the first *Stuart Little* movie that Hugh came to realise that his mind may not have been in the best of conditions.

Despite his often jovial on-screen persona, Hugh has always been quite a pessimist at heart, and it seemed the bigger and more successful his career became, so did the blacks clouds of depression that often shrouded his life in hopelessness.

From an early age, he had never been at ease with happiness of any kind; maybe it was his religious upbringing or maybe it was the effect of seeing his mother going through a similar kind of condition. Like her, he too suffered for long periods of 'heavyweight unhappiness', which began in his late teens and continued, despite all his success, his marriage and becoming a father. 'I train myself to look at the glass being half full but occasionally I slip. People often shout out at me in the street,

"Cheer up, it may never happen." You just want to shout back, "Fuck off, it already has."'

To the average Joe on the street, however, Laurie must have appeared to have everything going for him. His demeanour during interviews, when on occasion he looked bored and only entered the conversation periodically with a sharp comment or a knowing glance, portrayed an air of complete control. Looking back now, Hugh is convinced he used humour as a human shield to avoid getting too close to people. 'Making people laugh is sort of cowardly. It can be an intimate thing, but it also distances you from the person somewhat.'

Constant dissatisfaction with his achievements seemed to be at the root of Laurie's problem. He continued to think that there was something else he should be doing, some other activity that would make him happier. 'It wasn't that I couldn't talk about my problems,' he added. 'I used to bore my friends stiff. I'm amazed that people put up with it. I would cling to unhappiness because it was a known, familiar state. When I was happier, it was because I knew I was on my way back to misery. I've never been convinced that happiness is the object of the game. I'm wary of happiness.'

Open and honest, on his darkest days he felt totally crippled by his illness. Despite his increasingly popularity, he found it too much bother to even leave his bed at times. He was, he says, a miserable sod to be around. And no one suffered more than the people around him. 'I realised I needed to sort it out, that it wasn't going to go away on its own. I don't think I suffered any more than a plumber or a dentist would. In fact, dentists get it worse. They suffer from a very high level of depression.'

He accepts that his wife, Jo, and three children, Charlie, Bill and Rebecca, who were 13, 11 and 8 respectively at the time, were affected most by his condition. 'I diagnosed myself as being depressed and decided I would try and sort it out. I don't know enough about the illness to say whether it was clinical, but it was certainly more than feeling a bit sad. It went on for long periods of time and had all the other symptoms, like lethargy and not wanting to get out of bed in the morning. It's actually selfish to be depressed and not to try and do anything about it. I would cling to unhappiness because it was a known, familiar state.'

He soon began to realise things had to change for the sake of everyone. 'I can remember the moment when I realised I had a problem. I was doing this stockcar race for charity somewhere in the East End. But in the middle of the race, with cars exploding and turning over, life or death, it suddenly hit me that I was bored. I thought, "This can't be right. I should either be hating it with every fibre of my being or loving it because this is an extreme experience." I realised this was the state of mind of a depressed person.'

He woke up the very next morning and sought help. A close friend of his recommended a fantastic woman therapist. He found it incredibly helpful, if not a bit scary. Yet now he thinks that anyone who is depressed should seek help to find their inner peace.

'I went to therapy because I felt I had mislaid my joy, which is of no great note in somewhere like the US, but in England is a rather remarkable thing to do; the English don't do that.' He raised his eyebrows in mock disdain. 'Analysis helped enormously, and it affected my ability to perform because I just eased up a little. The thing that was inhibiting, the thing that was holding me back in terms of my work was the feeling that everything hangs on this. What happens in the next five minutes will determine everything, and it has to be perfect and nothing less than perfect will do. That, of course, is an impossible frame of mind to do anything, hit a tennis ball, tell a joke, anything. What this very brilliant woman [his therapist] allowed me to do was to see that that was a nonsensical frame of mind and that things just unroll, people's lives unroll. We go with things, we make mistakes, and we forgive ourselves for things.'

Hugh credits the time he spent with the psychologist as changing his life and giving him a new and fresher outlook on life. 'I know a lot of people think therapy is about sitting around staring at your own navel, but it's staring at your own navel with a goal. And the goal is to one day to see the world in a better way and treat your loved ones with more kindness and have more to give.'

He also jokes about his therapy. 'People are more open about seeking help these days,' he says. 'They recognise the fact that the alternative to having a shrink is that you bore your friends stupid. So I figured that I might as well give someone 100 bucks an hour to hear my woes. At least someone can make a living out of listening to my tedious problems,' he laughed. 'After 20 years, I'm still waiting to find a proper job.'

Refreshingly honest about his state of depression, he feels it's now in better control than it's ever been, but he also knows it is something that he will never really overcome fully. 'I wish I could say eating goat cheese or chanting helps, but I don't have any answers.' He adds, 'I'm happier when I know I'm on my way back to misery.'

He sadly, more than reluctantly, admitted that the depression may also have been connected to his brief extramarital affair with the film director with whom he once worked, but that was the only detail the star would go into. 'It possibly was connected. But I don't remember.'

On the bright side, his 13-year marriage survived the crisis and is now stronger than ever. 'It's terrific, and I'm very lucky. I'm so much happier now and more accepting of things. I used to get consumed with things that were in the past. I saw a million different versions of who I could have been and all of them were better. Why didn't I do this? Why didn't I do that? I look at my kids and I'm very proud that my wife and I created them.'

Maybe it's the fact he feels so uneasy with fame and hates being recognised. But that's the price he must pay for the profession he stumbled into all those years ago. 'People probably expect me to turn up in a Bentley with a shooting stick,' he grinned. 'I don't take off my motorbike helmet a lot of the time, that's one of the really good things about riding a bike. I can go all over the place and no one knows who I am.'

There were, in fact, several times when he admitted that he wanted to quit his erratic profession to see if it would help. 'You go to the edge and there's always something that tugs you back and you think, "Well, give it one more shot." It's not necessarily career things, I've been lucky and always found stuff to do, but there have been times when I thought, "Am I really cut out for this? Is this what I really want to do? Should I go off and become a teacher?" That's a valuable thing to do. Or "Should I try to write *Ulysses*…" but that's been done.'

'Perhaps it is a chemical imbalance,' he said. Although he won't take medication, he did once admit to resorting to the herbal remedy St John's Wort at a time of need, but it didn't work. He dislikes the idea mind-altering drugs.

Perhaps it's the fear of failure. It's keeping busy by doing a range of activities that seems to be Laurie's most obvious escape. But even that opens up fresh wounds on occasion as he looks to reach perfection in all he does. Although he claims he can't do anything very well. 'I think I'm a jack-of-all-trades and I'm sort of reasonably good at a lot of things but not great at anything yet. I'm a reasonably good writer. I don't write like Martin Amis, but I wish I did. But I can probably act better than Martin Amis. I can't act as well as Kenneth Branagh, but I can probably play the piano better than Kenneth Branagh, but I can't play the piano as well as Dr John. I may be able to cook better than Dr John. I rowed for Cambridge. I was pretty good at that.'

Although the ghost of depression hanging over him is fading year on year, he can now say, without the need to joke, 'I mean, who doesn't feel down? I get hungry every now and then, too,' he laughs. 'It's no big deal, really.' But he is cautious when assessing how far he has travelled from his darkest moments. 'Well, if life is a rollercoaster ride,' he said. 'I'm on a very straight bit at the moment. I don't feel those great triumphs and disasters that acutely. But I haven't had that many. I haven't stuck my name on something that's been a horrible failure. But, then again, I'm not Tom Cruise either. I sort of wish sometimes I had diplomas on the wall and was qualified to do something else, surgery of some kind. But I have nothing, not even an acting diploma.'

After many years he still attends sessions and he feels he is now a more pleasant and nicer person as a result. 'I am much easier to live with. So I can claim it's altruistic. I still catch myself going into moods sometimes, but the family is very good at dealing with me. They push me even further to provoke a resolution. So we have a short, heated shouting match rather than a protracted sulk. The depression is not nearly as bad as it was. I have a feeling I am through it.'

And he admits that having such great children has also helped to lighten his mood a little. 'They do make you less egotistical. I still manage to think about myself 98 per cent of the time, but at least there is a little window where others can impinge.'

After finishing *Stuart Little*, and with his mind still wrestling with his inner demons, Hugh moved way outside his comfort zone as far as acting was concerned. Without much persuasion he agreed to play the leading role in Christopher Monger's romantic comedy, *The Girl From Rio*, which required him to put on his dancing shoes.

'The script came through in a big envelope and I read it and thought, "this looks good fun", and it's also set in Rio which is a big plus. A very enjoyable project.'

On getting the role, he explained how in order to help him seal the deal he blatantly told a little white lie about one important element. 'I was actually making *Maybe Baby*; the producers were due to turn up in the lunch hour and we were supposed to have an hour talking about the movie and my character. But in fact they got held up in a bomb scare at the BBC, so they weren't allowed out of the building. In the end a guy ran in panting and said, "Dancing...can you do it?"'

Hugh explained that normally, being an Englishman, he would have ummed and ahhed for a while but there wasn't time for that so he just said, 'Yeah...oh, dancing fine...if you want any horse riding, umm pottery, archery, I can do any of that too.' He knew it would make the entire process quicker if he just lied, and it was only a little white one. In fact he didn't actually know what samba dancing was – he thought it was salsa.

In *The Girl from Rio*, Laurie plays Raymond, a downtrodden husband who is a Latin wanna-be dancing bank clerk who spends most of his time drooling over the cover of *Samba Monthly* and dreaming about the statuesque salsa dancer, Orlinda (ex-model Brazilian Vanessa Nunes), while hoping of one day escaping his drab life. After discovering his wife is having an affair with his boss, the easy-going bank clerk clears out the safe and hot-foots it to Rio. Once there, he meets chubby cab driver Paulo (Santiago Segura), who not only introduces him to the girl of his dreams, the exotic Orlinda, but also to the fringes of the Brazilian underworld. Like most comedies, it all finishes with a happy ending.

Writer-director Monger (best known for directing the quirky *The Englishman Who Went Up a Hill but Came Down a Mountain*, starring Hugh Grant) directed the movie. Along with Laurie, Nunes and Segura, it also stars Lia Williams, Patrick Barlow and Nelson Xavier.

After playing alongside the tall Geena Davies as Mr Little, Laurie again more than met his match in the equally tall Vanessa Nunes, who was a good inch-and-a-half taller than him when she was in her dancing shoes.

'She is gorgeous,' he duly mentioned in between takes. 'She's been terrific, and it's her first movie and it's in a different language for her. She's a real star.'

The dancing sequences in the movie did cause him some concern. On reading the script, he came across a line saying, 'Raymond's quite good, and when he dances he's transformed into this sexy man.' He swallowed hard and thought, 'Oh, no problem,' as he tried to picture in his mind's eye how the hell this modest man born in Oxford would suddenly be transformed into some kind of sex god by doing a dance. He began to wonder if he had done the right thing by agreeing to take on such a part.

'Stunt man.' He had a brainwave. 'They will probably use a stunt man to do the dancing.' But unfortunately for Hugh there was no stuntman; it was up to him to do it all. 'So I went to lessons on samba dancing and lessons on how to be sexy,' he shrugged.

Hugh found it incredibly hard to learn how to dance, even though he is a very musical person. The entire experience brought him down a peg or two when he found himself working with the dance experts who stood in front of him swaying their hips. 'I'm English...we don't have hips.' He remembers the hordes of people who applauded him on his performance, although he strongly believes they were only being kind. 'I believe that no man should dance,' he said, using his hands for effect. 'OK, some say, "What about Gene Kelly?"...OK, he got away with it...and Fred Astaire was sort of OK, and made it look less embarrassing than it might have been, but it's not a thing that men should do. They should sit at a bar and watch other people doing it, and then drive them home.' He added that men look good at playing cricket or playing football, but not dancing.

Samba schools in Rio are like football clubs in other cities. It's very competitive, and very, very serious. They even have their own colours. Hugh went to one school where he was called into a ring to dance with a stream of women. Claiming he felt a bit like a bullfighter, he said, 'I don't think I've ever been as frightened as the day, the first day, we shot a dance sequence in front of 500 professional Brazilians dancers, and drummers, and musicians...that was a very, very bad day.' He also said that when it was over he got very drunk.

As expected, he did conquer his fear of dancing and got the chance to work in one of the best cities on the planet: Rio, a place he had never really thought about before. Although he maintains he always had a passion for the Far East, getting to the heart of South America became a once in a lifetime opportunity. 'I had a terrific time. I felt like an idiot for not going there 20 years ago.' The city, like most cities, took a while to get use to. At first glance it appeared to be overrun by shoe shops and banks. But the more time he spent there the more he realised it was actually a very glamorous and exciting city, full of people looking to escape something in life. He found that working there, rather than just being a tourist, actually made it easier for him to plug into the Brazilian way of life. 'It was a great privilege to go and work there. Work is a quick way into a place, a way to meet people quickly, no small talk, straight away. Discussing inside leg measurements with a woman you don't know two minutes before. The more protestant souls amongst us would join the foreign legion, but if you can't stand that and having your hair cut short, go to Rio. A place where people go to reinvent themselves, may have robbed a bank to do it, or done terrible things, but it does happen.'

The film was charming and very funny and there was something about the plight of Raymond which really hit home with the actor: a guy escaping a drab life.

After the romance and sparkle of Rio, Hugh found himself in the city of Toronto, Canada to take on the tricky role as Vincente Minnelli, the husband of the world famous Judy Garland and the father of Liza Minnelli in an ABC Television TV movie in 2001 called *Life with Judy Garland: Me and My Shadows*.

The relatively expensive $12 million TV film recounts Garland's troubled life, a life and career marked by comebacks, highs and lows, financial problems, a suicide attempt and various broken marriages; it also delved into her intense bond with her children.

The film uncovers Garland's life from her early days of performing on stage as Frances 'Baby' Gumm at the age of two in Grand Rapids, Minnesota, up to her most famous role in the *The Wizard of Oz* and through the rest of her golden but tortured career at MGM, where she apparently worked nonstop and became addicted to the pills that eventually killed her.

It was based on the memoirs of Garland's own daughter, Lorna Luft, the half-sister of singer-actress Liza Minnelli, who also co-produced the film and was ever-present on the set in Toronto saying she had written the book because other biographies of her mother were inaccurate. 'I wanted to talk about Judy Garland as the person I knew her as, my mom,' said Ms Luft, who was 16 when her mother died. 'I didn't know her as an icon. I didn't know her as an idol. She loved her children more than anything in the world. Sure, maybe it wasn't a conventional childhood, but it was the only childhood I knew. We lived in hotels, we lived in houses, and we lived in apartments. I went to God knows how many schools. It was exciting and, yes, it was sometimes sad.'

Luft wanted to use the TV movie to dispel the big misconception about her mother being a tragic past-her-sell-by-date Hollywood figure. 'She wasn't tragic. She had tragedies in her life. But she had great optimism and a great sense of humour. And she knew how brilliantly talented she was.'

It also touched on the homosexuality of her father and a couple of her husbands, including the great director Vincente Minnelli, who Hugh portrayed in as witty a way as he could with such a frustratingly small amount of screen time.

The lead role for the part went to Australian actress Judy Davis, a smart and engaging actress who at 45 was only two years younger than Garland herself when she died of an accidental overdose of pills in 1969. Davies was well supported by Tammy Blanchard (Young Judy), Dwayne Adams (Mickey Rooney), Stewart Bick (Artie Shaw), Victor Garber (Sid Luft), John Benjamin Hickey (Roger Edens), Sonja Smits (Kay Thompson), Al Waxman (Louis B. Mayer), Jayne Eastwood (Lottie), Marsha Mason (Ethel Gumm) and Cynthia Gibb (voice of Lorna Luft).

With the help of make-up, Davis bore an uncanny likeness to Garland; she wasn't averse to playing the odd diva or two. Her past roles included Edith Piaf and Lillian Hellman, but she said that Judy Garland was the hardest role of her 25-year career. Weeks after filming had ended, she said she could not entirely free herself from Judy Garland.

'With Garland there's always a line you're frightened of crossing. It's daunting to play someone that talented. And whether she's just sitting there having a drink or whether it's hysteria, there's a line that you must not cross, because then you go into caricature and that's too awful to contemplate.'

Judy Davis confessed to getting unusually upset and on occasions breaking down while watching some of the scenes, especially when Garland realised that her managers had stolen all her money and that she was broke. 'It was upsetting because it was real, and she was also physically sick and obese and sick with drugs and I was relating it. This role demanded every part of me. She was bigger than me, much more talented with much bigger emotions. She was braver. So I had to get bigger to play her.'

Davis added, 'She was a tremendous pill abuser, she was known to take 40 Ritalin a day. She was a creature of great extremes. It's hard to avoid the reality of what was done to her at MGM when she was 13. Once they realised her effect on audiences and that she was brilliantly talented, they just worked her into the ground. The only time she had a holiday was when she had a nervous breakdown.'

The movie won plaudits for its gritty and sad portrayal of the Hollywood legend, bagging five Emmy awards including a Best Actress win for Judy Davis.

Hugh finally returned to the UK where he allegedly signed a half-million pound deal to make a comeback after a decade away from UK TV comedy, as actor and makeshift director in the ITV series *Fortysomething*.

An insider for Carlton TV said, 'We're thrilled Hugh is taking the lead role. It promises to be funny and sexy.'

The series was adapted for television from the novel by Nigel Williams. '*Fortysomething* is about marriage and growing older and, as more farcical and absurd events happen to these people, we wonder how they will survive,' the writer explained.

Hugh looked glad to be back on safe ground after a long while travelling around the world. 'I've not done anything on TV for a very long time, so I thought it's now or never. I'm going to be dead in a minute, so what am I keeping myself pure for?'

Hugh played the troubled GP Paul Slippery, an anxious husband and father who is beset by the tribulations of oncoming middle age and feeling increasingly confused by his family and the world around him. He struggles to understand the sexual shenanigans and rivalries of his three sons, who would leave Casanova exhausted. And what makes it worse is that he can't remember the last time he had sex. To add to it all, his long-suffering wife Estelle, played by *Four Weddings and a Funeral*'s Anna Chancellor, has decided to go back to work. The show also starred Neil Henry, Joe Van Moyland and Benedict Cumberbatch.

Anne, who plays the long suffering wife of Hugh's character, was more than pleased to be portraying a kind, understanding wife and mother after playing a string of domineering women such as Miss Bingley in *Pride & Prejudice* and Henrietta, or 'Duckface', in *Four Weddings and a Funeral*. 'Estelle was much more in the realm of playing myself than many roles I've had. It was nice for me to play a part where I could wash my hair, put on a bit of make-up and say "Good morning. How are you?" I could be a mum, which is something I understand.'

'It's a jolly, farcical comedy,' says Laurie, 'but it does have underneath it an anxiety about when you reach this point in your life – your children are growing up, you are established in your career and then you ask, "Now what? What am I here for?" His character can't remember the last time he had sex, and finds his wife and sons very confusing.'

Married with three children, like Slippery, Laurie laughs off any comparison with his character in the TV show and feels he is nothing like the neurotic small-screen alter ego Paul Slippery, who is struggling to cope with the male menopause. 'My experiences wouldn't make a six-hour television show for a start,' he says. 'I suppose I'm more bemused rather than panicked. I'm not as neurotic as Paul. Friends of mine might disagree but I think of myself as vaguely puzzled by life rather than neurotic. Also my own children are younger than Slippery's. I've still got the teenage years to come. But I'm just starting to get a glimmer of it, with the odd door slamming starting to raise its head.'

In reality, Hugh is quite adamant that being the lazy person that he is, he just can't be bothered with the small petty stuff. 'I just get bored with it after a while.' As for reaching the forties, he shrugs. 'On the whole I think we all worry too much. I think now is a good time to for a man to be in his forties. We're not fighting in the trenches in northern France, there's no bubonic plague ripping through the streets, there are all sorts of things we must not lose sight of. Generally we live more comfortable, healthier, disease-free lives than we have at any time in human history.'

What's more, he said that when reaching the big '4-0' he was relatively neurosis-free, although it did take him about three years to get used to it. 'It took time for it to sink in,' he says. 'I still had that teenage feeling that there was lots of time to do the things I wanted to do and then suddenly I found myself grunting as I got out of a low chair, and you think, hold on, I'm not 17 any more, I've got to get on with stuff.' He added, 'If I do worry about anything, it's whether myself at 40 is a betrayal of what I'd hoped I'd be at 20, or whether at 20 I was just a callow youth, and whether looking back, I'm more embarrassed at me at 20. When I was 20, I thought by 40 I'd have opened the batting for England, climbed Everest and written a cello concerto. So I've probably let the side down.'

Fortysomething gave Hugh the opportunity to direct once again after three directors walked out for a variety of reasons, some personal, some professional. 'The directors kept pulling out and as the weeks went by there was a danger the plug would be pulled altogether. They left for a variety of reasons,' explains Laurie. 'But who knows? It was all about logistics, scheduling problems, nothing too sinister. Certainly I don't know, all of it happened without my involvement or knowledge and it was slightly alarming when you see the captain of your ship jumping past your porthole,' says Laurie. 'The producer asked me would I consider stepping into the director's chair, and for some reason I agreed to it. It was a big challenge, and I suspect the very stupidity of it made it more appealing.'

Hugh stepped up to the director's chair without a second thought although it wasn't all plain sailing. 'I wouldn't recommend it,' he says. 'It was insane and very misguided. It was rewarding in some ways and certainly exciting but only in the same way that a car crash is exciting. I did it because the very stupidity of it made it appealing. If it had been easier, if someone had said I had three months to prepare and I could change whatever I wanted, I probably would have said no. There was something about the very insanity of it that made me say yes.'

Fortysomething also saw Hugh baring his soul, and his behind, in front of the camera yet again. 'I had a nude scene in *Fortysomething*. It lasts two seconds but it felt like a lifetime. Slippery is following his wife out into the street wearing a towel, keen to discuss matters of a sexual nature,' explains Laurie, 'and a passing dog, you know how this happens, it's happened to all of us, a passing dog steals the towel. I didn't find it embarrassing at all,' he continues, his face expressionless. 'I was obviously careful with the hand gestures,' he says with the beginning of a smile. 'I would tend to use just one hand at a time. I never went, "I want those two trucks moved!" But, yeah, it was rather stressful. The dog was slightly hard work. We'd actually filmed this scene before under one of the previous directors, and that time the dog had behaved very well, he was a very good actor. But in the meantime, and no one told me about this, he'd been castrated. Chaps, I can assure you it's not a way to go if you want to be focused on your work. It took a lot of vim out of the dog and he lost his edge. He was fine but he took a lot of coaxing.'

He expanded further on the nude experience: 'I spend far too much time in the series without my trousers on. It wasn't embarrassing at all.' All of which left both character and leading man distressingly vulnerable, especially when Laurie was required to carry on directing the scene as though everything were completely normal.

When news of Laurie's stint of naked acting and directing was suspiciously leaked, a tabloid photographer attempted to enter the street to take some candid shots, but luckily for Laurie they were kept at bay. 'We also strove to avoid school chucking-out time,' he recalls. 'It's not the kind of thing you want to film with a dozen 16-year-olds laughing from the other side of the street. It's meant to be in Wimbledon, but we actually filmed the scene in Crouch End, very appropriately named.'

One onlooker who was lucky enough to witness some of the action said, 'Hugh gave us all a bit of a fright, but he was having a great time of it. He didn't mind who saw him.'

His next project, *The Young Visiters*, aired during the 2003 Christmas season. It was a BBC Edwardian drama written by nine-year-old Daisy Ashford in 1890, who apparently wrote a chapter a day between breakfast and bath-time, and delivered it to her parents in a stout two-penny exercise book 12 days later. Hugh said, 'I play a melancholic figure called Bernard Clark who mopes around a castle in dressing gowns being tragic.'

Clarke was Daisy's idea of a romantic hero. The role also called for Hugh to play the piano and sing the one song in Bernard's repertoire, a little ditty about how unworthy he is. Laurie added, 'It's a song about self-flagellation and he sings it frequently.'

Daisy's only living daughter, Margaret Steel, took a shine to Hugh when she came to visit the set. 'He's just how I imagined Bernard Clark,' she commented.

He also got the opportunity to brush up on his rowing skills when in one scene his character proposes to his girlfriend on a boat. 'It was difficult to get a motor on board,' Hugh muttered, 'so, like a fool, I said I'd row, with eight crewmembers aboard. That was a very long afternoon.'

The film was well received and showed just how talented and astute Daisy Ashford was to write something like that at such an early age. It went on to win a BAFTA for Best Original Television Music, plus it was nominated for several other awards including Best Actor for Jim Broadbent.

'There's an intelligence to them [House and Wilson] I like. I mean, Hugh has it, he's one of the few guys I can throw Bob Newhart references around and he knows what I'm talking about. Or Lenny Bruce.'

Robert Sean Leonard, Dr Wilson in *House*

CHAPTER 12

'A FEW BOMBS IN THE
F***IN' POST'

It could have been the hours he sat in his trailer waiting to be called on to set, the influence of one of his all time heroes, P.G. Wodehouse, his avid love of reading, or perhaps he was just looking for somewhere to place all the crazy thoughts spinning around in his vivid imagination that made Hugh decide to write his first novel.

Whatever the reason, Hugh had spent all of his life surrounded by books and falling head first into their pages. He recalls the many books and authors that shone brightly in his memory. 'I remember not just the books themselves but the chair I sat in, the shoes I wore, the woman I loved, what song was on the charts at the time.'

He quotes *The Grapes of Wrath* by John Steinbeck, *Moby-Dick* by Herman Melville and *Catch-22*, by Joseph Heller among his favourite books of all time. In typical Laurie style, he explains that his inspiration for *The Gun Seller* wasn't as dramatic as any of the above. 'I sort of fell into it. I started writing a diary because I thought it was something one should try. Then I got bored with my own life, my average day seems so dull, that I started making things up. It became fun. I got carried away and wrote a book by accident.'

If anything, the experience proved Hugh wasn't afraid to stick his head up above the trenches for the world to take pot shots at him. He must have been fully aware that actors or pop stars who dare cross over into other art forms are often slaughtered by every man and his dog. 'I wrote the first one strictly for me and when I submitted it to a publisher, I did it under another name. I wanted to get a sort of fair reaction that had nothing to do with my name, such as it is.'

The Gun Seller, published in 1996 by Penguin, UK, showed another side to the talented Mr Laurie. His aim, before he penned the novel, was to write a series of six novels because he believed that it was the only way to show the world that he was a serious writer. 'I wanted to write them under a different name but my publisher said, "Do you know how hard it is to sell any book anywhere without you mincing around behind a veil of secrecy?"'

The Gun Seller is an extremely well-written thriller spoof with shades of an offbeat James Bond adventure, touches of a Robert Ludlum plot, and the often surreal outlook of *The Hitchhiker's Guide to the Galaxy*. Laurie playfully takes the main character Thomas Lang, who is approximately Hugh's age and IQ, reluctantly on a journey into the murky world of international terrorism mixed with high-tech gadgets, beautiful models, fast motorcycles and Bond-style scenery. Lang, ex-military, is a good person who happens to ride a motorcycle and whose life is in a bad way. Somehow, along the journey he gets roped into this bizarre but hilariously funny adventure. Lang is self-effacing and sharp but has lots of panache and often shows his human side. Not dissimilar to one Gregory House, but since *House* came almost a decade after *The Gun Seller*, it is fair to say that the character is closer to the creator than anything else.

The actor-author insists, however, that there is nothing autobiographical about this first novel except the murder, mayhem, intrigue and high-speed car chases. 'This is fantasy. I can produce fantasy, I live on fantasy. It's a thriller with jokes. And I made a choice between writing a serious novel, my attempt at the great novel, and writing six cheap and cheerful novels. And I went with cheap and cheerful, but I've still got five to go.'

Like all good authors, Hugh researched diligently to ensure that the plot was accurate and realistic, especially concerning the use of guns. He happily admitted to being completely ignorant about how the gun world operated but that he needed to find out because he himself hates books that don't go into detail about the subject, like writing *Jaws* and being too lazy to find out anything about sharks!

The writing process was gruelling and Hugh says he suffered from painful periods of writer's block during the dark nights of burning the midnight oil. He attempted various methods and creative techniques, including keeping a journal of his time to get his imaginative juices flowing. Again, he struggled through it and though he claims he's not a perfectionist, Laurie admits he can sometimes worry a project to death. 'In some areas I'm positively slapdash, slipshod.

Then I can find myself obsessing over something and redoing it and redoing it and redoing it. Writing, I do it so much to the point that I've disassembled the thing so many times that I'm unable to reassemble it. I've actually killed projects, my own things. Things were ready to go and I just pull it apart again and go, "Oh, it's broken now." It's very depressing.'

Mentally drained when he finished, he still commented that he much preferred the process to acting, 'because you can do it lounging on a pillow rather than running upstairs 14 times. But I'm a very shallow person and I'm simply attracted to the idea of sitting there in some Bloomsbury way.'

Obviously nervous about how the book would be received, Hugh basically kept it to himself and showed it only to those who needed to see it. He didn't even let his best friend Stephen Fry cast his expert eye over it, although he didn't need to worry because when Fry finally did read it, he simply said, 'The funniest and most charming novel I have read in years and years. If you see someone howling with laughter on the subway, sobbing with joy in the street, or exploding with delight on an airplane this year, it's because they're reading *The Gun Seller*.'

The book critics agreed and gave it the big thumbs up, all commenting on how well he blended the comedy and suspense into some truly hilarious moments.

With the release of the book, of course, there were many comparisons made with more famous authors especially some of Hugh's favourite spy writers, John Le Carré, Ian Fleming and Tom Clancy. Although Hugh was more than happy to be mentioned in the same breath as such excellent writers, he stated that he didn't intentionally copy anyone's style of

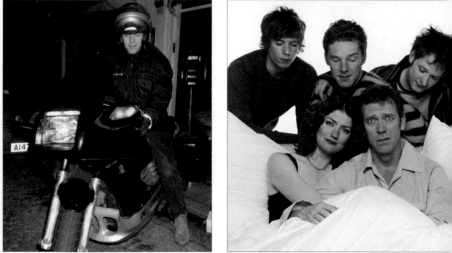

Above: Hugh with friends Lenny Henry, Dawn French and Ben Elton in 2003.

Below left: Motorbikes are one of Hugh's great passions – he loves being able to ride around incognito thanks to his bike helmet.

Below right: The cast of *Fortysomething*. Hugh played Paul Slippery, an anxious GP coming to terms with the onset of middle age, and also directed the series.

Above left: A musician as well as an actor, Hugh appears at a 2004 fundraiser at the Oxford Playhouse.

Above right: Sporting the first signs of that Gregory House stubble, Hugh looks surprised by the number of adoring fans who turned out for autographs after his appearance on *The Late Show with David Letterman* in 2006.

Below left: Hugh with Dame Helen Mirren at the 2006 Emmy awards. *House* was nominated for Outstanding Drama Series but lost out to *24*.

Below right: Looking every bit as irascible as his character – Hugh pictured on the set of *House* in 2008.

Hugh has been
catapulted to global
stardom thanks to
his role as Gregory
House, MD.

Above: Turning his hand to music once again at the Netflix LIVE! summer concert in Los Angeles in 2008.

Below left: Hugh at the 2009 People's Choice Awards, where he scooped Favourite Male TV Star for the second year running.

Below right: Hugh's status as a Hollywood superstar means he now attends all the swankiest showbiz parties – including the Golden Globe Awards. *House* has been nominated for six Golden Globes and has won two, with Hugh picking up the Best Performance by an Actor in a Television Series in 2006 and 2007.

Above: The cast of *House* at a party to celebrate 100 episodes of the hit TV series.

Below left: Hugh toasts more success at the 2009 Screen Actors' Guild Awards.

Below right: The Hugh Laurie millions worldwide have come to know and love – a long way from the bumbling characters he was known for at the beginning of his career.

Hugh's global fame means that he is in demand all over the world, appearing on talk shows in the USA and Britain and even as an animated version of House in US comedy series *Family Guy*.

Never one to be typecast, Hugh
lent his voice to the character of
Dr Cockroach, PhD in the smash
hit film *Monsters vs Aliens*.

Hugh Laurie has truly had an incredible career, playing characters from lovable English buffoons to the dark and complex Gregory House. He is sure to be a major star of film and TV for many years to come.

writing but admits that *The Gun Seller* is more in the tradition of a P.G. Wodehouse than anyone else.

After publication, Hugh soon began to revaluate his original goal of a six-book series. 'This is it. This is the only one, the first and last. I found it very pleasant writing *The Gun Seller*, but it was very scary to put it out in front of the general public. Authors are generally given certain latitude on the first book they publish. The second time is harder.'

The Gun Seller's success in the book charts ensured strong talk of adaption into a screenplay, with the rights held by MGM, and production by John Malkovich's production company. 'I sold the rights to a producer,' said Hugh, 'who then sold them to a studio who then asked me to write the screenplay. So there I was, the cheque virtually still in my hand thinking, "I've sold the rights and it just won't work", and then they come and ask me to do it and I have to say, "Yeah, right, easy". In fact it's proven bloody difficult.'

John Malkovich, the actor, was excited about the project although he knew it was going to be a tough battle to get the right amount of finance for the film. 'It's incredibly hard to find financing. It takes a long, long time.' John said he was under no illusion that the industry would give him an easy ride just because he was a famous actor. 'I think credibility just comes from having a cheque book; it's just the way the business is. There's no point in crying about it.'

After lots of negotiating over many expensive lunches, the right backing was secured only for the project to be abandoned around the time of the 9/11 attacks on the Twin Towers due to the terrorism elements in the story. 'It's at the bottom of the pile now. I was working on it for about two years, which is a shame, but people lost a lot more than I did, so it's one of those things.' Disappointed, Hugh still hopes the movie will be produced in the future but denies rumours that he will star in the role of Thomas Lang, even though he is now much older than he originally envisioned the main character to be. 'In some fantasy world I suppose I did write the character for myself. But the reality is that it's a big expensive film with a lot of explosions and it's going to need a big American star. A tadpole.'

An audio-taped book was also discussed but, again, for various reasons, that didn't see the light of day either. On the bright side, *The Gun Seller* was finally published in the United States (after previously being rejected for being 'anti-American') to critical acclaim with comments like 'A first-rate thriller...an awesome entertainment machine... a smashing book.'

Years later, everyone is still waiting with bated breath for the second book. 'My second novel will be coming out two years ago,' joked Hugh when asked about the follow-up. 'I'm on my second book now and I'm finding it quite hard. I enjoyed writing the first one because it was just for pleasure. Now people are expecting it, I'm quite nervous. This one will also be a thriller featuring guns and car chases. I'd like to write a serious book but I'm not grown-up enough.'

Laurie was rumoured to have written the second book, *Paper Soldier*, which he also considered naming *The Man in the Ironic Mask*. Amazon.com announced that the novel would be published in mid-September 2007. However, as the date came and passed, Laurie's agent announced that it was a mistake on Amazon's part and that Laurie had not even written the novel yet. Amazon then stated that *Paper Soldier* would be published in September 2009, again a date that was not to be met.

'Though I've been working on a sequel for ten years now and feel terribly guilty for not completing it, I'm eager to make some amends to my publisher and the two or three fans who have been waiting so long and so very, very patiently,' Hugh explained.

However, while the wait continued, Laurie wrote a TV pilot script for CBS, *The Dragons of New York*, which was filmed but not picked up as a fully fledged series. 'It's a shame because I still have a real fondness for it. But that's the nature of things in the US right now. If you're not making *CSI* you're in trouble. I'm still learning the intricacies of the business here.'

In January 2009, 13 years after the original English publication of *The Gun Seller*, a French translation of the novel entitled *Tout Est Sous Contrôle* (Everything's Under Control) was published by Sonatine and later topped book charts in March 2009 in France, becoming a surprising bestseller in the country.

Hopefully success in a country like France, which is not known for accepting anything English, will be the spur Hugh needs to once again start writing 'his diary' and give his legions of fans the other five, or at least the second, of the books he promised. But who knows? He explains, 'Part of the situation with me is that my fantasies are so vivid it stops me from doing things because I feel like I've already done them. I never, ever thought I'd make a career out if this fantasy and play-acting. In fact, I'm still waiting for a proper job to come along.

'I've never had any compulsion to express myself, actually. There's nothing conscious or premeditated about it. I just meander, trying my hand at different things. I don't enjoy a lot of things that others find fun. But I do have fun working, and the enjoyment often comes rather incidentally from that process.'

Some would now say that Hugh's first 'proper' job was just around the corner, but there was a plane, a desert and 'that' audition to do first.

In 1965, an adventure film about a cargo plane that crashes in the Sahara desert entitled *The Flight of the Phoenix* was made by Robert Aldrich, director of *The Dirty Dozen*. It starred Jimmy Stewart as the captain pilot and an all-star cast that only the Hollywood of the 1960s could have put together, including Richard Attenborough, Peter Finch, Ernest Borgnine, Ian Bannen and Hardy Krüger, who played an eccentric German engineer. It's basically a story about the triumph of the human spirit against all odds. A group of air-crash survivors are stranded in the desert with no chance of rescue. Facing a cruel environment, diminishing resources, and the possible attack by desert smugglers, they soon realise that their only hope is to do the impossible and construct another aircraft out of the wreckage of the plane.

The remake of the classic film, made in 2004, starred Dennis Quaid in the role of Captain Frank Towns, the pilot whose C-119 plane is full of oil workers returning home after shutting down an oil field in Mongolia's Gobi Desert. The plane suffers the same fate as the original, with a new batch of passengers left to try and escape from the heat and danger of the desert. As well as Quaid, who found it amusing to wander around on set doing his best Jimmy Stewart impression, there was Giovanni Ribisi, Tyrese Gibson, Miranda Otto and, of course, Hugh Laurie, who takes on the role of Ian a stiff-upper-lipped army captain played in the original film by Peter Finch.

From the outset, director John Moore was confident that he had made the right choice in deciding to remake a classic that starred a hatful of very famous Hollywood superstars. 'It's just a fucking great story,' John explained, 'I know it is a risk, it's Jimmy Stewart for Christ-sake and people do have this fondness for it. I'll get some hate mail, a few bombs in the fuckin' post. What are you going to do?' Yet Moore confesses to never even having seen the original. He just knew that if a story's worth telling, it's worth telling again. 'There's an interesting visual metaphor, they are lost at sea, on a life raft. That opened it up for me. The desert is an ocean. If someone wanders away they are dead.'

Moore insisted on certain dynamics with the cast and wanted to create a mixed bag of diverse characters to represent life's leftovers. 'The point for me is not that they are lost. It's that no one can be bothered to go find them.'

When the film got the go ahead to 'take off', there was a long line of actors queuing up to spend a few months camping out in the heat of the African desert. 'It went round the usual sort of Hollywood madness,' says Moore of the process of casting for the movie. He swears that Tom Cruise wanted to do it, but he wanted Dennis Quaid. 'He's like Kevin Costner, he can play tough guy who will kick your arse and have a fucking searing intelligence about them. I would have walked over broken glass for Giovanni and Hugh Laurie. And the rest, it's just this perfect shape.'

As usual, a modest Laurie claims he had no idea why someone would pick him to go to the desert and star in an adventure film. 'It was clearly a typing error on the part of the film-makers, but when I turned up on set and fitted the character's clothes, I got the job.'

The film was shot on location in Namibia, South-West Africa, in the coastal dune belt which follows the coast for as far as the eye can see. Cast and crew were all encamped among the massive sand dunes for four months, and the sand was getting on everyone's nervous.

'It's a pain in the fucking arse,' muttered the director from Dundalk, Ireland, who is known in the trade for being 'a bit of a character'. Moore spent a lot of time driving around in a colourful quad and swearing as good (or as bad) as a trucker in a traffic jam. Niceties and general adjectives were not on top of his list when trying to direct the $45-million budget movie. 'Honestly, it's a fucking quagmire. I've seen grown men weep just moving lights and cranes. You get into that fable of *Lawrence of Arabia* thinking they sat on a shot for 12 hours until the light was right. It's probably bollocks.' As well as conquering the art of swearing, Moore also got an 'A' in losing his temper, which he did often during the making of the film and on numerous occasions quite violently at the cast and crew of the film.

With the intense heat and hostile conditions of the desert, Hugh soon realised it was a crazy place to actually be travelling through, never mind attempting to make a movie in. 'One doesn't grumble, being English. After all, we invented the desert,' he said shrugging. 'It would be unseemly for me to moan. It has been hardest on the crew. People have dropped because of the heat. Meanwhile we sit under parasols playing cribbage and eating dates. No surprises about sand for me; it should be kept in those little glass eggs.' Hugh, whose Scottish Presbyterian upbringing often surfaces in these situations, added, 'So many of us wander through life in a sort of frothy cappuccino of comfort and ease. To be brought up against hardship when you're not used to it.' But as the wind and sand sailed past him and the night closed in, he just puffed out his cheeks and grunted, 'This is a maddening and frustrating place to be, isn't it. And can someone tell me how the Namibian desert is fucking colder than Aberdeen.'

While they were waiting for some of the equipment to arrive, disaster struck when the ferry carrying a major set piece sank in the river during transportation, causing hours of work in retrieving the piece from the bottom of the river. On top of this, Moore's plan to build a fully working Phoenix plane fell foul of the authorities, who had major safety concerns after a similar type of plane crashed during the filming of the original 1965 film, causing the death of stuntman Paul Mantz. This meant that Moore had to use a model of a Phoenix for the final end scene instead.

Four different versions of the same aircraft were used during the film; a Fairchild C-119, a direct descendent of the WWII era C-82. A Phoenix that could be taxied manually, but not flown, was built for close-ups. In the remake, the Phoenix flying scenes were done using a radio-controlled model and computer graphics. The model used for the crash sequence cost $250,000 and was so perfectly built it actually flew further than the crew and testing had predicted. In fact, it flew so far it hit the camera filming it and broke the cameraman's leg.

Unfortunately, this was not the only accident on set: Jared Padalecki flipped his vehicle and luckily survived even though at first everyone thought he was dead.

Hugh also had an accident of sorts while playing a few fun games in between filming. 'We were making a movie about people abandoned in the middle of nowhere. One night four of us were sitting on top of a 100-foot dune, looking at the moonlight, and we decided to somersault all the way down to the bottom. I went first, got to the bottom and suddenly said, "My wedding ring is gone." The other guy's were tumbling down and I yelled, "Stop! I've lost my wedding ring."

'It was dark, two o'clock in the morning. You immediately think if it's anywhere near you and you move, you're going to bury it. The four of us started searching, and within about 20 seconds one of the guys halfway down the dune yelled, "Is this it?" I said, "Of course it is. How many wedding rings are you going to find here?"'

By the end of filming they were all glad to leave the heat and the sand behind them.

The reviews for *The Flight of the Phoenix* weren't good, with critics saying it was too similar to the original. 'If you've seen the original, there's absolutely no difference in what happens. And very little reason to check it out.' Possibly the most scathing review, however, came from an aviation source, *Aerofiles*. In their aviation film-review section, they stated, 'The cast is purposely unlisted here to spare them any further embarrassment. Perhaps the worst remake ever of a classic film.'

Meanwhile, Moore was upbeat about the longer-term prospects for the new movie. 'Nobody likes to get beat up. But the first film was a flop when it came out and now people speak of it as a classic. I hope a similar fate awaits me.'

As far as Hugh was concerned, he came out of the film with credit and took another step upwards in his 'unplanned' career. And importantly, it was the film that changed his life. Or, rather it was his one-off audition with his haggled weather-beaten features after four long months of making the film in the desert which helped change his life forever.

On finally leaving the desert after several months, he was asked if he enjoyed the experience and if it had helped him discover anything about himself? True to form his answer was as honest as ever and coated with a hint of sarcasm. 'I didn't discover anything about myself. I discovered lots about other people, but nothing about myself. It's always the way.'

'Guilt I can do. If I have any expertise at all, it's in the area of guilt. I have a black belt in guilt. If you ever want a guilt-off, the next time we meet let's see how we match up. I'm pretty confident in that area.'

Hugh Laurie

PART 3

IS THERE THE SON OF A DOCTOR IN THE HOUSE?

CHAPTER 13

'SO WE GAVE
HIM PAIN'

'I was a fan of his comedy, but I honest-to-God never thought he'd be right for this role.' So David Shore, creator and head writer of *House*, admitted when he heard Hugh Laurie might be auditioning for the project. 'I was thrilled. Not because he was perfect, I didn't think there was a chance he would do this. I just thought he was hysterically funny and it'd be a thrill to meet him.'

Nevertheless, the writer's preconceived impression of the comedy star was about to change for ever when the English actor walked into the room. Although Hugh's physical appearance was not exactly how Shore had pictured House to be in his own mind, he instantly thought he would be right for the part. 'He read the part far and away better than anyone else did. But deeper than that, he actually came in with an understanding of the character.'

The TV show, *House*, was Shore's newborn baby and he

was afraid that in the wrong hands the lead character would just appear hateful and mean and very unlikeable. He was looking for someone who could do these horrible things and be somehow likeable without just 'petting a kitten'. The search was on for an actor who could deliver both the humour and the seriousness of the situation at the same time.

'It's a really tricky, difficult role, and he could come off on-screen as just a hateful jerk. Hugh got all the nastiness; it was all there, yet at the same time, you came away liking him. You sympathised with him and wanted to watch him. There was a reality to it, not cartoonish.'

Executive producer Katie Jacobs recalled how tough it proved to cast the role because of how complicated the character needed to be. 'If he didn't have a gravitas, you wouldn't believe in his intellect. If he didn't have a sense of humour, you'd think he was an asshole. If he didn't have pain and wasn't wounded behind the eyes, you'd never forgive him.'

She remembered seeing a long list of actors who auditioned for the role, but none of them really got close to achieving what they really wanted out of the role. 'Then we saw Hugh, and everyone agreed he had both. He made you laugh without losing the significance of what he was talking about.'

David Shore had a string of hit shows on his writing resumé from the past 15 years including *Law & Order*, *Family Law*, *The Practice* and *NYPD Blue*, among others, so he wasn't a stranger to drama TV. Nevertheless, *House* was still a new experience for him in that he was the main creative writer and not just part of the writing team. The thought and responsibility excited him and scared him half to death in equal measures.

The concept for the show, which originally had the working title, *Chasing Zebras, Circling the Drains*, came about when he and executive producer Paul Attanasio heard that there was some interest in a medical procedural show, a bit like a *CSI* but with doctors, set against the backdrop of a hospital. As a result, armed with a ballpark idea and a stack of little-known diseases taken from the *New York Times* magazine's diagnosis column under their arms, the pair decided to pitch their proposal to the people at Fox.

'We knew the network was looking for procedurals and Paul came up with this medical idea that was like a cop procedural. The suspects were the germs. But I quickly began to realise that we needed that character element. I mean, germs don't have motives. We're looking to create the same thing that most shows are, drama and an opportunity for people to examine various ethical issues.'

Once given the go-ahead from the studio, they set out to find the right director to make their vision come to life. That director came in the shape of Bryan Singer, who had directed features films such as the *X-Men* trilogy, *Usual Suspects* and later the *Superman Returns* movie. 'It was such a pleasure as a writer, having a director who you'd hear talking to the actors about what was going on in this scene, and what the character is all about. And he identifies stuff in my own work that I didn't know was there. I'd say, "Yeah, that's good that works really nicely." He really, really got the material,' said Shore.

While Singer had made a name for himself in the Hollywood film industry, he was more than keen to try his hand at television and saw directing *House* as the perfect outlet to explore this type of media. 'I'm a bit of a hypochondriac and quite fascinated with the medical world and very much adore the character of House,' he said. 'I don't want to say I'm like him, but I can see moments of myself in him. Depending on how you look at it, this could be a worrying self-revelation. House is about as far removed from the good family doctor as one could get.'

Next up was the difficult job of assembling a first-rate cast that would be good enough and experienced enough to give the writing the justice it deserved. It was then that Laurie threw his hat into the ring and not only bowled them over with his facial expressions and the glint of humour in his eyes but his fake American accent, as mentioned, was so convincing that it even fooled Singer. The story of his audition and its reaction is now the stuff of legends.

Shore and Singer had already seen loads of actors, including many from England. Bryan especially got very tired of it all when the actors either couldn't get the character right or couldn't sustain the accent for a long enough period of time. Singer was so pissed off that he swore he wouldn't waste any more of his time looking at 'foreign' actors. The next day they got Laurie's tape in the mail and Singer said, 'Why can't we see more actors like this?'

Apparently Shore waited for several days before telling Singer where Hugh was actually from. The director had no idea that the guy he was putting on a pedestal of everything American was actually Brit. 'I saw the tape and he did a flawless American accent and he was all shaggy and unshaven and he kind of just jumped out of the screen.'

With Singer, Shore and the rest of the writing team all singing Hugh's praises, it was then left to the little matter of convincing the people at the Fox Network that the 45-year-old Englishman, who had made his name mainly playing comedy parts, would be the right person to ensure their investment paid dividends.

The production company naturally had some reservations, but in the end they happily went along with the decision of the director and the writer and Laurie got the gig. As a matter of fact, he was the final actor to join the cast of *House*.

'The script really didn't change that much after he came on board,' Shore said. 'What he did was he made it work. It's very easy to sit in a room and write "The character is tall yet short, crusty yet lovable." But you want characters who are complex and tricky and who have characteristics that are self-contradicting; it's much easier to write that, than to act that.'

The next tough hurdle to overcome was getting through the pilot stage and beyond without getting pulled by the network. It's a dog-eat-dog world in the land of pilot shows, with over 80 per cent not making it past the first stumbling block and sometimes even then still getting canned for poor ratings.

Everyone involved knew it was going to be a particularly tough task to get the audience to like a character who is outside the norm of what they were used to – a straight-talking lead man in the guise of a doctor who is also a patient-hating maverick.

'That was always a concern,' Singer says. 'But to me, I felt as long as he's good at what he does and he's saving lives and he's got those Hugh Laurie eyes, then he could get away with anything.'

Even today, Hugh still reckons that putting such a mean, unsympathetic character at the centre of the show was an extremely bold thing to do, especially a person with such an antisocial coat covering him that he doesn't think twice about upsetting patients, colleagues or the powers-that-be alike; extremely bold, foolish, or a stroke of pure genius?

Needless to say, many of the highly rated and successful US shows are based on a large ensemble cast of actors with complicated stories – *Lost*, *Desperate Housewives* and *CSI*, to name just a few. Meanwhile *House* is centred mainly on House, and without him there would be no show. But the writers were aware that they needed a support cast to add the extra spice to the mix. The original team comprised *Dead Poets Society*'s Robert Sean Leonard, *ER*'s Omar Epps, *Neighbours*' Jesse Spencer and *Dawson's Creek*'s Jennifer Morrison, with Lisa Edelstein playing Dr Lisa Cuddy, all with an excellent pedigree and experience.

Lisa Edelstein was born in Boston in 1967. She trained to be an actor at New York University's Tisch School of the Arts and performed in numerous Broadway productions, including the AIDS-related musical *Positive Me*.

In *House* she plays Dr Lisa Cuddy, the Dean of Medicine at Princeton-Plainsboro Teaching Hospital. 'I think the writing is so smart,' she said, obviously pleased with the way her character is portrayed in the hit show. 'And I love the snappy dialogue that my character has with House. I like their relationship.'

Apparently it was Singer who chased her and sent her a copy of the pilot script after enjoying her portrayal of a prostitute on *The West Wing*.

Today Edelstein lives in Los Angeles in a century-old home with her pets, her cat and rescue dogs. She is an avid practitioner of Ashtanga Yoga and volunteers her time by working with the Best Friends Animal Sanctuary, Save the Children, Planned Parenthood and amFAR (The Foundation for Aids Research).

Before *House*, she worked in a variety of medias including stage, film and TV. One of the reasons she was picked for the role was her ability to successfully play a host of fearless roles over the years. These include playing Rob Lowe's call-girl girlfriend on *The West Wing*, the transsexual boyfriend of James LeGros on *Ally McBeal*, David Conrad's lesbian sister on *Relativity*, an Orthodox Jew losing custody of her child on *Family Law* and James Spader's love interest on *The Practice*.

She also has guest starred on *Frasier*, *Seinfeld*, *Felicity*, *ER* and *Without a Trace*. On the big screen she's popped up in films such as *What Women Want* with Mel Gibson, *Daddy Day Care* and *As Good As It Gets* alongside Jack Nicholson, plus many others. Edelstein has also done lots of voiceover work, from *Mercy Graves* to the animated version of *Superman* and the *Justice League* series, as well as guest spots on *American Dad* and *King of the Hill*.

'Right from the pilot we had really good banter, which was what got me hooked. I never expected to be doing this with my career. I always assumed I'd be doing toothpaste commercials,' Lisa added.

Robert Sean Leonard (Dr James Wilson) was born in New Jersey but now lives in LA with his wife, daughter and two dogs. He began acting at the age of 14 at the Public Theater in New York. At 19, he made his film debut in the acclaimed *Dead Poets Society* starring opposite Robin Williams and Ethan Hawke. He also starred in *Much Ado About Nothing*, *The Age of Innocence* and *Mr & Mrs Bridge*.

He has had a distinguished career on stage and was a three-time Tony Award nominee (1993, 2001 and 2003), winning in 2001 Best Actor in a Featured Play for his role as AE Housman in *The Invention of Love*. Two years later he was nominated again for his performance in *Long Day's Journey into Night*, which also starred Brian Dennehy, Vanessa Redgrave and Philip Seymour Hoffman. He also played Romeo in *Romeo and Juliet* at the Riverside Shakespeare Company in 1988.

Leonard's career has also spanned a number of classic films, alongside such great actors as Daniel Day-Lewis, Christian Bale, Paul Newman, and Denzel Washington.

In *House* he plays Wilson, head of the oncology department, and appears to be the only true friend to House. He received the script for the CBS show *Numb3rs*, at the same time as *House*; he liked the *Numb3rs* script and thought it was 'cool' and planned to audition for the show. However, he believed that the character he was up for, Charlie Eppes, was in too many scenes, and he later stated, 'The less I work, the happier I am.' At the same time, he auditioned for *House* and knew it hadn't gone particularly well and that his past friendship with Singer may have helped win him the part of Dr Wilson. 'I didn't want to be the lead guy. That's too much work. But I thought that it might be fun to be the lead guy's friend. I'd have days off and still get a pay check every week. Hugh Laurie, who plays House, is remarkable. I lean in the door and say, "Hey, what do you think about egg salad for lunch?" Then I have two days in a row off. It's a great gig.'

Omar Epps (Dr Eric Foreman) was born in Brooklyn, New York in 1973. Before he started acting, he formed a rap group called Wolfpack with his cousin in 1991. He began writing screenplays at the age of ten and attended the Fiorello H. LaGuardia High School of Music & Art and Performing Arts. He gained fame in movies like *Juice*, *Higher Learning*, *Love and Basketball*, *In Too Deep*, *Alfie* and *The Wood*. In 2004, Epps landed the role of drug-dealer-turned-prize fighter Luther Shaw in the biopic *Against the Ropes*.

Epps was nominated for an NAACP Image Award (presented annually by the American National Association for the Advancement of Colored People to honour outstanding people of colour in film, television, music and literature) for Best Actor for the original cable movie *Conviction* in which he portrayed Carl Upchurch, a hardened criminal from South Philadelphia who spent most of his adult life in prison. He formed a production company, Brooklyn Works Films, where Epps worked as writer, producer and star of many of the films they have made.

Epps was no stranger to appearing on medical shows; he played Dr Dennis Gant on the Emmy Award-winning drama *ER*. In fact, he was involved in one of the most talked-about series exits, when he left the audiences wondering whether his character had just left or committed suicide. 'Before *ER* a lot of people knew my name and some people knew my face. I saw a big difference after *ER*, like, wow, I didn't know television was so powerful.'

On *House*, he plays Dr Eric Foreman, a neurologist, winning him a NAACP Image Award for Outstanding Supporting Actor in a Drama Series in both 2007 and 2008, and nominations in the same category in 2005 and 2006. Epps also lives in Los Angeles, and is married to singer Keisha; they have two children.

Jennifer Morrison plays Dr Allison Cameron, an immunologist in the show. She too felt that her audition for the part had been a complete disaster and was unaware that Singer had watched some of her performances, including *Dawson's Creek*, before her audition and had already pencilled her in.

Morrison was born in Chicago and raised in Arlington Heights, Illinois. She was destined to be a star from an early age, appearing in print advertisements for JCPenney and Montgomery Ward as well as commercials for Rice Krispies and Mondo. At the age of ten, she was featured on the cover of *Sports Illustrated for Kids* with basketball star Michael Jordan.

She studied at the famous Steppenwolf Theatre Company in Chicago and earned a degree in theatre from Loyola University. At 15 she made her film debut as the daughter of Richard Gere and Sharon Stone in the 1994 film *Intersection*, and later appeared as Samantha in *Stir of Echoes* with Kevin Bacon in 1999. She went on to take the lead in the 2000 film *Urban Legends: Final Cut*, and has since gone on to appear in films including *Grind* with Adam Brody, *Surviving Christmas*, *Mr & Mrs Smith* opposite Brad Pitt and Angelina Jolie, *Warriors* and *Star Trek*. She also added producer to her CV, with the independent film *Flourish* in which she also starred.

Recently she was nominated for a 2008 WIN Award (Women's Image Network) for Outstanding Actress in a Drama Series for her work on *House*. She now lives in Los Angeles.

Australian actor Jesse Spencer's agent suggested that he audition for the role of Dr Robert Chase. Spencer wasn't all that interested, believing the programme was going to be similar in style to *General Hospital*, but he changed his mind after reading the scripts. After he was cast, he persuaded the producers to turn the character into an Australian.

Spencer grew up in Melbourne, Australia, and like most good-looking actors in that part of the world, turned up in the soap opera *Neighbours*, playing the role of Billy Kennedy for six years from 1994 to 2000. He has since appeared in the drama *Death in Holy Orders*, as well as the films *Winning London*, *Uptown Girls* and *Swimming Upstream*. He's also done some stage work in *The Modernists* and *Peter Pan*.

Spencer had been living in the US since 2004 when he got the role in *House*. During the show, he and Jennifer Morrison got engaged after apparently meeting at the Vancouver International Airport where they were on their way to film the first episode of *House*. The engagement was called off in 2007.

At the end of season three, there were a few changes to the original cast when House dismisses Chase, while Foreman and Cameron resign. House forms a new diagnostic team, which he handpicks from seven finalists. The producers originally planned to recruit two new full-time actors, with Foreman's return, bringing the team back up to three members. Ultimately, three new regular cast members were agreed on as well as Foreman. House's new recruits were new doctors Lawrence Kutner (Kal Penn), Chris Taub (Peter Jacobson), and Remy 'Thirteen' Hadley (Olivia Wilde).

With a strong cast in place from the start, it was doubly important to ensure that each episode was well written with a dramatic edge and that the medical facts that revolved around the core of the show each week were accurate and believable.

The writers, with little or no medical background and knowledge, wisely decided to enrol a specialist, a person classed as 'the expert' with the technical know-how required to make sure the audience believed the stars of show, the one's in the white coats (or sneakers and cane), looked and talked like the real deal. 'There's a doctor named David Foster who works with us on the show. He was credited with the title of executive story editor,' said Shore.

The technique they used to write each episode was quite unique to many of the writing team. They would start with some mysterious disease they found hidden away in some medical journal. Then they would find out about its symptoms, and then proceed to write the plot from there. 'To some extent we work backwards. We start with the disease and then work back through to the character of Dr House,' said Shore. 'The title diagnostician of the show would be as smart a physician as Dr Kildare and as sharp a sleuth as Gil Grissom of *CSI*.'

The outcome of each episode saw House and his team presented with a new mysterious illness to solve while in a foot race against time to save their patient. House in particular is often seen peeling away at the disease like an onion while keeping his distance from the patient until enough of the mystery is uncovered to solve the ambiguity crime. 'If we can stumble upon a symptom we haven't used before, that's great, because obviously we can't end every act break with a seizure,' says Shore when asked about this dramatic way of storytelling. 'But usually what we've found is that it's less about the medical story and more about the person who is sick. It really becomes about the personalities involved and what that can reveal about House and the rest of the doctors.'

However, a good medical television show needs more than a bag full of exotic disease with unpronounceable names. Singer was looking for more. 'There's a procedural element to it, sure, but if all House did was cure a disease every week, he'd get boring pretty fast.'

So the original idea for the show, based solely on medical mysteries, soon changed and evolved as the writers focused more and more on the title character, spinning the show around him. Shore traced the concept for the title character to his background as a patient at a teaching hospital. 'I knew, as soon as I left the room, they would be mocking me relentlessly for my cluelessness and I thought that it would be interesting to see a character who actually did that before they left the room. Everybody has idiots at their job, and those idiots are talked about when they leave the room. House just calls them idiots before they leave the room.'

Shore admits that there is a lot of himself in the character and traits of House and agrees with almost all of his view points, although he admits that he hopes he doesn't have the cynical and cold attitude lurking within the doctor. 'House is a rebel,' added Shore. 'I have a rebel inside me that will probably be there when I'm 80. I also share many of the opinions and attitudes of the character, including his cynical streak. But it's not about what House says; it's about what he does. He's heroic, but he doesn't care what people think. Like Hugh and myself, House is a big believer in rationality and truth over emotion. He is able to tell someone to go to hell, and that definitely has a universal appeal. We can all identify with the feeling that we're surrounded by idiots and we're the only one who gets it, but House gets to call a moron a moron.'

Laurie's character, with the unlikely title of the Chief of Diagnostic Medicine at the fictional Princeton-Plainsboro Teaching Hospital, is portrayed as a medical genius and a loner. Around him is a cast of doctors and managers who find themselves often in conflict with his unorthodox diagnostic approaches.

The peculiar notion of a doctor who saves lives but hates people was the concept the creators were searching for. 'I used to be an attorney,' Shore said. 'And I would still be an attorney if I didn't have to deal with people. I think human interaction is the most annoying feature of most jobs. So I started thinking of a doctor who hated patients and when I began embracing that I came up with [Sherlock] Holmes.'

Shore credits much of the inspiration for the now famous cantankerous doctor to Arthur Conan Doyle, the creator of Sherlock Holmes. A huge Sherlock Holmes fan, Shore unashamedly dipped into world of the famous fictional detective to not only mould House in a similar image but also to set the tone for the medical mystery show. The resemblance is evident in various elements of the series' plots, such as House's reliance on psychology to solve a case, his reluctance to accept cases that don't interest him, and even his home address: House's apartment is 221B while Holmes lives at 221B Baker Street. Other similarities between the two characters is their frequent use of drugs, with House being addicted to Vicodin and Holmes recreationally taking cocaine, plus the use of a cane, playing an instrument – Holmes the violin and House playing the guitar, piano and harmonica – and, of course, a talent for accurately deducing people's motives and histories from aspects of their personality and appearance.

Shore also explained that the name 'House' is a play on the name Holmes (i.e. 'homes') and that both Holmes and House have one true friend: Dr Watson for Holmes and for House, Dr Wilson. Leonard has said that House and his character were originally intended to play the roles of Holmes and Watson in the series, although he believes that House's team has assumed the Watson role as the series progresses.

'The original idea of the show was House and Wilson, like Holmes and Watson,' Leonard says. 'But it got away from that, and his team is Watson, if you want to be technical about it. I think it's good, and when it's right, when the show works, the mystery works. It has a Sherlock Holmesian feel to it and you do kind of want to know what's wrong with the patients. And it is interesting, the turns and twists that get you there. And there's always a little bit of character-driven fun stuff in between, of who these people are and how they affect each other. And that's it at its best. And I guess that could be true of any show.'

Shore also draws inspiration from Dr Joseph Bell, who was Doyle's major source for the creation of Holmes. Doyle had met Bell, a Scottish lecturer, in 1877 and went on to serve as his clerk at the Edinburgh Royal Infirmary. Doyle described Bell as a person who apparently could walk into a waiting room and diagnose people without speaking to them. The links went even deeper when in the finale to season two, 'No Reason', House is shot by a man named Jack Moriarty, a name that coincides with Sherlock Holmes' adversary, Professor James Moriarty; similarly, in the fifth season, Wilson uses Irene Adler as the name for the make-believe love interest of House, the same name as the only female enemy Holmes ever bumped into.

'Holmes was a drug addict, like House, and House's best friend's name is Wilson. So, it's like Holmes and Watson, House and Wilson. Robert Sean Leonard plays Wilson and he's one of the only friends that House has,' said Singer.

'It's the Holmes-Watson thing we were hoping for,' said Katie Jacobs, on pairing Leonard with Laurie. 'The chemistry of the two of them is so brilliant that it's something we spend a lot of time with now.'

One of the many ideas batted around by the creators from the start was to get the audience to see that this man who cured people had his own share of pain, both mentally and physically. They agreed to give him some kind of disability. Shore added, 'I wanted House to be damaged emotionally and to have a physical manifestation of that. I didn't add that to soften him, I didn't want to soften him. I didn't set out to make him sexy. I just wanted him to be interesting. We needed a reason why people would find a nasty, antisocial doctor likable,' said Shore. 'So we gave him pain.'

Initially, House was to be in a wheelchair similar to the 1960s police drama *Ironside*, but luckily Fox turned down that idea, which everyone involved with the show is now really happy about.

'As originally conceived, we had him in a wheelchair,' Shore recalled. 'Fox said, "No way." They were right. It works better to show him at the same level as everybody else, but in pain with every step. This is a guy who doesn't have time for niceness or pretence,' said Shore. 'He wants to get to the stark truth as quickly as he possibly can.'

The wheelchair turned into a scar on his leg, a scar from an injury so bad it caused a limp and required the use of a cane.

'House usually holds his cane on the same side as his injured leg,' Shore explained. 'Some people feel more comfortable with the cane in the dominant arm, and that is acceptable.' Later on in the series Hugh began to perform tricks with the cane out of boredom.

For Laurie, the limp made it extra complicated getting into the role. 'Oddly enough, it's not his physical gait that is transforming. It's being one-handed. I find it actually much more constricting than walking with a limp. To be one-handed, to drink a cup of tea and put two sugars in and open a door and answer a telephone, becomes incredibly time-consuming. Every scene for me is about where am I going to put the cane. When I pick up this, where am I going to put the cane?'

He admits that on occasion he limps with the other leg, not to throw viewers off but to preserve some kind of pelvic symmetry, which he says is number one on his list of life goals. 'If I spend 15 hours a day throwing it out one way, I feel I have to redress the balance. My colleague, Stephen Fry, back in England, volunteered to come on the show. He said "I have no character ideas, but what if I had two limps?" I thought that would be an entertaining addition.'

House creator David Shore dismisses any idea that the series was out to capitalise on pain. He was just looking for a storytelling device. 'We wanted a character who was unpleasant, so we made House the victim of a crippling, embittering blood clot.'

'House presents a certain bravado and genuine irreverence', Jacobs said. 'But the closer you get to that face, the more you see what's going on in his head and behind the eyes. I think every woman in America wants to heal him'.

As a by-product of his leg problem, and as a clever way to make him appear even more damaged and flawed to the audience, the Vicodin addiction was added, an addiction which House himself refuses to admit to when challenged about it. 'I do not have a pain management problem, I have a pain problem,' he often says.

'We wanted him to have things he was dealing with, and an addiction is certainly interesting and made sense,' said Shore who applauded Fox for not stepping in and trying to change the concept. 'They've been great with a character that a lot of networks would have easily said, "He's too rough around the edges." They completely embraced him.'

As well as his addiction to pain killers, and apparently the odd soap opera, each episode quickly exposes House's deep-seated dislike for any form of interaction with his patients. 'He's a bit acerbic and breaks a lot of the rules that have been established in decades prior in terms of your sympathetic, humanistic medical examiners or ER doctors,' Singer said. 'He's in it for some other reason, some deep, dark personal reason, but he also happens to be quite brilliant at it. It makes him quite fascinating and an endless resource for character development.'

From the very start of the first episode, it is obvious to all that House is a very strong non-conformist with little or no regard for how others perceive him, while showing utmost contempt for anything to do with authority. 'House enjoys pursuing the truth, and he knows we all see the world through our own lenses. He's constantly trying to strip himself of those biases, to get a clean, objective view of things,' added Shore.

He doesn't wear a white coat, maybe subconsciously, so patients don't recognise him and bother him with their problems. Instead he dresses informally. In fact, he dresses down as one would expect Hugh Laurie himself to dress when not working – T-shirts, sneakers and jeans.

To get that image just right, Cathy Crandall, costume designer for the show, created the look. She went for the wrinkled T-shirt, a blazer that is one size too short, faded and worn-in jeans and heather-grey rag socks. The sneakers were apparently Hugh's brainchild, with the basic logic of 'a man with a cane needs functional shoes'. The sneakers became such an essential piece of footwear for Laurie that the wardrobe department at Fox studios keeps 37 pairs of Nike Shox on hand. On the show, House has also worn famous brand T-shirts such as Barking Irons and Lincoln Mayne, but he's also worn shirts by less known designers such as Andrew Buckler and Taavo. Apparently the trick is to keep them tied in a ball overnight to give them that worn-in look.

In the show, the character of House speaks English, Spanish, Portuguese, Hindi, Japanese and Mandarin. With hints of the real Laurie, he is also an atheist who openly and relentlessly mocks colleagues and patients who express any belief in religion.

Shore was more than pleased on how Hugh aided the writers and the writing process simply by his presence and his range of talent. As the character progressed, Laurie brought elements to the character that weren't originally on the page. On occasion he plays guitar, duets on the piano, juggles and even skateboards. 'Hugh frees you up to write almost anything. You can have the most dramatic, heavy, emotional scene, and you can throw a one-liner in the middle of it, and he'll pull it off. People will laugh, and yet you'll still have all that emotion, which is really unbelievable. Hugh's comic timing absolutely fuels the show. We can give him the most outrageous things to say and he says them and somehow they're dark but they're also very, very funny.'

Hugh relishes his role as House, and it shows as he seems to effortlessly become the character, one of the most fascinating TV antiheroes of all time. 'It is absolutely thrilling to have licence to say things that perhaps we all think from time to time but feel constrained not to say,' said the British actor. 'To be able to make observations about your fellow man is a great freedom and a very enjoyable thing to do, particularly when it's written in a way to make me sound more much intelligent and learned than I actually am. There are many things about being Dr House that I find instinctively comprehensible and I sympathise with his grumpiness.'

Even with his experience as the son of a doctor, it was only in his role as House that Hugh really began to understand what doctors have to put up with day in day out, and the whole situation nags on his brain. It's also the fact that being an actor makes him appear more useless at these things than most. 'There is a definite skill to this because most of the time I'm almost embarrassed by how skill-less actors are. I mean, here we are pretending to have this enormously profound medical knowledge and expertise when, frankly, the cast of *House* could scarcely put on a Band-Aid without reading the instructions.' He is deadly serious at the thought. 'And sometimes actors can feel rather ashamed of that. We're rather ashamed that we can miss having a concrete skill, a concrete expertise that can save lives or build bridges or explain the world.'

Like House, Laurie is slightly suspicious of alternative

medicine. 'I am very sceptical, and that has got a lot to do with my reverence for my father and for his belief in the rational, logical and empirical,' he says. 'I don't find herbs, acupuncture, and the mysteries of the East all that enticing. I've gone to an acupuncturist and put drops of herbal remedies in my bath and done all that sort of stuff. So I'm a bit miffed with our current love affair with all things Eastern. If I sneeze on the set, 40 people hand me Echinacea. But I'd no sooner take that than eat a pencil.'

If just a little set in his ways, Hugh also pictures House as somewhat of a heroic figure. A man who is willing to give up friendship and make sacrifices in search of some kind of truth, whether it's scientific or psychological or whatever. He says, 'I really do think of the guy as a hero. He's not polite. He's not somebody you'd want to take home to meet your mother, necessarily. But he is in search of truth and that truth one day could save your life or the life of someone you love. I'm not saying I would want to be him or could be him, but I do think he's heroic.'

Hugh doesn't necessarily think of him as a pain in the ass, just someone who likes to do his own thing, someone who doesn't care whether people like him or not. 'I envy that. He's not a good man all the time. He's complicated and frequently obnoxious character, which I find is part of the fascination. This is not about your typical TV angel.'

Deep down, Hugh has said that he wouldn't have any problem with having a doctor like House look after him in real life. 'If your life is hanging, or the life of someone you love, is in the balance, of course you would withstand any amount of abuse to get the job done and to get the life saved.'

And Laurie is not alone in his willingness to be treated by House. A recent TV guide poll showed that bizarrely 36 per cent of respondents named Gregory House as the television doctor they would most want by their gurney in an emergency.

It's quite obvious that Laurie and House have lots of similarities. 'We both look at the world with one eyebrow arched. We're both quite serious but also have a childishness. He and I are eternal adolescents but with this morbid gravity. The other thing is, we both have issues with joy, in so much as we think it's beyond us. I often picture that scene in the Woody Allen movie when he's on the train and looks into another car that's full of people laughing. They're drinking champagne, somebody has a trombone. And Woody is very much on the outside of that, looking in. I'd say that sums up my view of the world, as well as House's.'

As the first series took shape, it was his more than credible American accent that filled up more newspaper columns than probably anything else at that time. But if rumours are to be believed, it could have been much different. After casting Hugh in the role, they did consider making House English, but it didn't last long. Hugh recalls, 'They did let me try House with an English accent, for about 12 seconds, before Brian Singer said, "Thanks that's enough."'

Acting is tough enough but acting in a strange accent is mentally exhausting. It was no different for Laurie, as speaking differently for large chunks of the day proved extremely draining. 'It's as if you're playing left-handed. Or like everyone else is playing with a tennis racket and you have a salmon. And I feel like there is a small elf just throwing pebbles at my face, one at a time, every time I come across a word with the letter R in it,' Laurie says, sighing. 'It's distracting and painful, and, now and then, one gets me in the eye.'

He still finds it immensely tough and he struggles to check himself every day, every scene, and every sentence. 'One part of my brain is doing it,' he explains, 'and the other part is listening all the time. It's true of all my life. I wish I could silence that part of my brain. Or remove it. I still have good days and bad days. On the bad days, I'm really struggling with the accent. Anything with an R is a big problem. Federal court order is very difficult. Coronary artery is almost impossible. My heart sinks every time I see a scene with those two words in it, and afterwards I have to lie down in a dark room for about 20 minutes. New York, oddly, is a nightmare. The most difficult is any speech in which I have to repeat a word. You can never predict which ones will be the problem. There can be other reasons for it, depending on what you had for breakfast or whether you slept well. Suddenly you can't say the word 'table', never mind encephalopathic hyperinsulinemic. The first time I tried to say that one I got a nose-bleed.'

Although most people are unanimous that his accent is flawless, he jokes that to him it sounds like 'A touch of Hungarian and Pakistani, depending on how tired I am.' But he also adds that it doesn't make much difference because 'I often find that a lot of Americans don't have good American accents either. So that's something of a relief.' On occasion, when he is being criticised by Americans for his fake accent, he is quick to point out that at least it's not half as bad as Dick Van Dyke's terrible attempt at a British accent in *Mary Poppins*, which Hugh states 'Was tantamount to an act of war!'

Regardless, Hugh constantly works to develop his

pronunciation when on set and, as much as possible, during the week he tries to stick with his US accent and only goes back to the English version at the weekend.

What doesn't help him is that American TV is far more demanding than British TV because the season is three times as long. 'It's a similar work schedule on British TV, but we only make six shows. Being on a show that goes on for nine months, that is a strange concept for an English actor. I've never worked this hard, but the fact is I love it. Of course, there have been some days where the thought of taking off for Rio has become very appealing.'

Yet for all his put-downs, he definitely carries it off more than adequately. 'I think it's because people know too much about actors in their home territory. One of the reasons I got the role of House is, coming from England, I was largely unknown to Americans. There were no preconceived notions or expectations about how I was supposed to look or sound. I was new, and that was attractive. But the British are wise to me. Any sort of linguistic affectation drives the English absolutely mad. I mean, we are a nation of Professor Higginses, and we're all out to detect falsehood and artifice in the way English speakers speak.'

Robert Leonard, who plays Wilson, is an actor used to playing characters with different accents. He says Hugh's got it a million times worse than anything he's ever had to do. 'It's hard when you're in a play, doing the same lines, the same way for eight months. Hugh learns 72 new lines a day and has to put an American accent on them. It's really is an actor's nightmare. I've done [with accents] Brian Friel plays, Martin Sherman plays, Tom Stoppard plays, and maybe five months into it you have a night where you kind of feel OK and kind of forget the accent and let go and let the scene happen. To have a strange accent in your mouth while playing a role, and then be judged for it, that's hard stuff.'

The reviews of the first series were positive. Tom Shales of the *Washington Post* called House 'the most electrifying character to hit television in years.' A writer in the *Seattle Times* gave 'three reasons to watch the show: Hugh Laurie, Hugh Laurie and Hugh Laurie'.

The series itself won an Emmy for best dramatic writing and although Hugh didn't win he was nominated that year for best actor in a drama series; James Spader took the honours instead for his role in *Boston Legal*. 'For the show to win, that's a much better thing. For an actor's own vanity, of course, it's a wonderful thing to be picked out, but for the show it's a much more important, it's a much bigger thing,' Hugh commented.

Bryan Singer, who was used to measuring success of his films by the takings at the box office, got a surprise taste of the shows growing success by accidently eavesdropping while at an airport. 'When I was flying back to America for the holidays, there was this kid who was coming home from college and his parents were picking him up at the airport. He hadn't seen his parents since the semester began and the first thing he's telling them about is this new medical show with this abrasive doctor! This is all happening five feet away from me as I'm getting my luggage. I almost said something, but then I was like, "Oh, they'll think I'm crazy." But I actually got to hear the word of mouth about [my] show right before my eyes.'

Fortunately, the words at the baggage carousel translated into much bigger ratings figures in the US and *House*, a show originally only given 13 episodes, finished its 22-episode season as one of 2005's biggest hits.

Hugh was more downbeat. 'I still think it's a terrible mistake they made. I have smacked the set many times cursing them for not hiring an American actor. American actors have natural selves that are appealing. They've usually got a pleasing pair of eyebrows or a nice voice or a nice something. I don't have any of that. I'm not easy on the eye or the ear or anything else so I have to come up with something which one could loosely describe as acting.'

His own modesty and the way he constantly put himself down was not lost on the people around him. 'It's predictable,' said Katie Jacobs, the executive producer of *House*. 'Every day at about 4 or 5 o'clock, Hugh's sitting on the kerb completely despondent. I tell every director before they start, don't think it's you, it's him! He's miserable no matter what he does. Never thinks he's good enough, never thinks he's got it right.'

'I had 20 years of being a clown and a buffoon and it's very odd to have another crack at it, to start all over again in a different country. It's a real blessing because not many people get that opportunity. In a way I feel I've slightly squandered it. I should really have done something more radical and be wearing silk fedoras and snakeskin shoes by now. I came to America as a faceless new person, and I've enjoyed that, I must say. To be able to pretend to be something that I'm, frankly, not is very liberating and exciting – it's a whole, sort of second, bite of the apple.'

Hugh Laurie

CHAPTER 14

'I'M JUST IN A FERRARI OF A ROLE'

In terms of the impact of the new series on American TV, *House* got off to a reasonably good start with series one. It included the Emmy Award for the writers, plus good solid reviews from most of the critics and a loyal and growing band of followers.

'I have almost no perception of anybody watching the show,' Laurie confessed. 'For at least a year I had the sneaking suspicion that actually there was no film in the camera and we were just doing this as a tax loss for somebody.' He added, 'But in truth I didn't think the show would be such a success. Okay, I thought it would fail. Not because it was bad. I was confident it was good, but plenty of good things just sort of wither on the vine. I thought I would have an enjoyable and interesting three weeks of filming in Toronto and maybe I'd end up with a one-hour tape I could show my friends and be proud of. Then it's, "We think we're going to do six now."

"Wow, six?" Then six became 13 episodes pretty quickly, then another five, then another four after, then whack! Twenty-two. Now it's, "Oh, my God, I'm a heroin addict and didn't even realise it!"'

The explosion in popularity all happened so fast that Hugh and everyone who lived the *House* suddenly found their lives, both on and off the screen, taken to a new level.

'The show started out a bit slowly, but Fox stuck with it because we believed in it,' says Peter Liguori, president of Fox Entertainment.

Not only did they stick with it, but they pulled off a masterstroke when the second series was neatly positioned into the slot straight after one of the biggest shows on American television, *American Idol*, headed up by another British superstar, Simon Cowell.

Almost overnight, by giving the show what is called in TV land a 'lead-in' it was propelled into the top ten shows and its viewing figures jumped incredibly from an average of 6.5 million per week to touching 17 million, an increase of around 150 per cent. Viewing figures doubling overnight is a rare occurrence on US television.

A brand new audience both young and old were exposed to the show. Executive producer Jacobs was surprised at its success. 'We had a core of fans who had discovered us on our own before the *Idol* move. But we never imagined we would have this huge an audience.'

Hugh fully believes that in the early days what people liked about the show was that it wasn't rammed down the audience's throats or thrust into their faces. It wasn't marketed to death like some other shows, covering every inch of billboard space. He feels that because the fans 'discovered' the show themselves, they excitedly told their friends and family about it.

'Well, it was very gradual. In the first year we went unnoticed. I mean, nobody watched,' said Laurie. 'It wasn't until we followed *American Idol* in season two that it started to pick up. Then we had some very big episodes, like our 'Super Bowl' episode when 30 million people were watching, and that's when things got really strange. People want to know everything about you.'

The speed of success and the commitment required to make a second series reportedly forced Laurie to pull out of the big budget movie, *Superman Returns*, directed by Bryan Singer, in which Hugh was to play Clark Kent's editor, Perry White.' That was a disappointment,' he said. 'That movie will just be huge, but it's great that we have a second season too.'

Even Singer, who was upset about losing the actor he wanted for his film project, still couldn't quite believe how fast *House* climbed up the ratings. 'When I left the country early in the series the ratings were up to 14 million,' he said. 'We finished the season with about 20 million. We got a boost because we came on right after *American Idol* but we kept climbing from there, which was really, really terrific.'

With the second series hitting new highs, and a third series already pencilled in, the pressure of suddenly being out of work at the drop of a hat was relieved. It allowed everyone, writers and cast, to relax more and really start to develop the plots and the characters.

'It's not about the freedom to do other projects,' said Hugh. 'It's the phenomenal quantity of this one. It's hard although I feel very lucky to be doing this. There are few things on this earth that are so enjoyable that you want to do them 16 hours a day every day, week in, week out. It's tough, but that's what it is and I'm not going to complain.'

Hugh found it hard to explain how all of a sudden his face was appearing all over the place. 'I don't know the secret of success. I don't even like to mention the word because if I do,' he looks up, 'someone will drop a piano on my head. I have no sense of anyone watching it. I'm not sure it's even on the air. They show me these pieces of paper with numbers on them and I can't make head or tail of them. They say, "We've gone up five per cent in the left-handed six-year-old vegetarian market, which we are excited about." They gave me one yesterday with the numbers for the show that went out on Tuesday night. There was only one number I could see that increased and I got really excited. It turned out to be the date.'

As *House* went from strength to strength, everyone heaped lavish amounts of praise on the British star for the part he'd played in creating such a success; praise which he was more than happy to deflect in other people's direction, especially Shore and the rest of the writing team who worked so hard behind the camera. 'I'm just in a Ferrari of a role,' he says. 'Mickey Rooney could win an award playing House. They, all of them, work incredibly hard to make me seem clever and heroic, neither of which I am.'

It is so well written in fact, that he has said that he doesn't struggle with all the emotional stuff expected of him by what is written on the page. 'I actually don't. For the most part, I play it as written because these scripts are exquisitely well done. Every week we have a read-through and David Shore asks if we have any thoughts. All I say is, "Print it on blue paper and it will be much prettier." That's about all I can say! It is a blast to read the scripts. My wife reads them for fun because they're so great.'

Behind the camera the crew and cast couldn't quite make out the behaviour of their main star. It shocked them that Hugh worked so hard, rarely said no or complained when he was tired, even though he often worked over 60 hours a week. He was a rare breed of leading actor who displayed gentlemanly manners and genuine modesty.

Katie Jacobs, executive producer of *House*, sees many similarities between Laurie and his television alter ego. 'He is incredibly smart and quick and funny the way that House is. I think a large part of why the character works so well is because, although House is really abrasive and arrogant and caustic on the outside, as an actor, Hugh Laurie lets us see inside of him and brings that inner life out, so that you forgive him because you see so much going on there on the inside.'

Shore was another one taken aback by Laurie's relentless work ethic and constant development of his character. 'Hugh makes us see the heart in the character, even without saying anything, even while saying the most outrageous things,' he says. 'He's always in pursuit of what's right for the character and the story. He can do funny in the middle of a dramatic scene. He can do dramatic in the middle of a funny scene. We've never come up with an idea or a scene or a line that Hugh cannot do.'

Of course the modest British actor is just as quick to dismiss the praise as 'lies, all lies' but concedes that he takes his work seriously. 'What I do is put all my heart and soul, if I had a soul, actually, which I don't. I travel light in that sense, into doing it right, getting the scene to play the way that it should. I don't see that there's a lot of House in me or the other way around. So I'm not losing myself in the character, exactly, but I do get lost in the intricacies of timing and tempo and connection,' he says. 'I'm rather obsessive that way.'

The other actors also sing his praises as they realise Hugh's portrayal is one of the biggest reason for their continual success. Jennifer Morrison is amazed by Hugh's dedication. 'You know, for Hugh, it's not just showing up and saying a few lines. He's saying medical terms constantly, and then, along with the accent, he's got the limp and the figuring out how to handle all the props because he's only got the use of one hand. He's constantly juggling and that's a lot to think about when you're just trying to act.'

Leonard is also full of praise for his co-star. 'I show up every week and do 8 scenes, while Hugh does, like 40. I would shoot myself in the mouth if I were him. There are a lot of adjectives for the character House, like cantankerous and curmudgeonly. That's all great, but it's very tiring unless the person's enjoying it.'

Another thing which impressed Leonard was Hugh's ability to unofficially co-direct certain scenes. 'It's not an exaggeration. He really does say, "Are you cutting from that shot to this shot? Because if so, that would be awkward. Are you kidding me?"'

When asked about this, Hugh shrugs and speaks quietly. He knows he is a pain in the ass. 'I have tried to exert an influence, and as the show grows in its success an increasing burden is placed on, no, that sounds sort of pompous, I meddle. I meddle in other people's business. Because I care. I care whether it's this prop or that prop, this shot or that shot, this colour or that colour. I'm sure there are plenty of times when they wish I would just shut the fuck up and say what's on the page.'

Jacob paints him in a very different picture of the 'meddling' star. 'I don't experience him as a meddlesome. He has all these great ideas. And he is, quite plainly, a genius. But I think he sometimes feels reluctant to share his ideas. He gets in his own way. He never gets in our way.'

Shore agrees. 'I watch him sometimes and I'm amused because I know what he's doing. But he's trying to not let anybody know he's doing it. And half the time people don't even realise he's done it.'

In the autumn of 2006, as a side line to the show and as a pleasant distraction, Hugh got to host one of the most influential American TV shows of all time as far as viewers, and more importantly as far as street credibility is concerned, *Saturday Night Live*. In the US anyone who is anybody is only somebody if they have appeared on the cult comedy programme. He stole the show with hilarious skits and musical performances.

The same year he also appeared on *Inside the Actor's Studio*, legendary for its in-depth interviews by host James Lipton, where he talked about his life and loves and also played around a little on the piano.

Even before his *Saturday Night Live* performance, *House* had already become a big hit with the younger generation who liked the sight of the rebellious doctor wandering around without a white coat and going head to head with authority.

In fact he won the Teen Choice Award. 'How about that?' he said, 'I'm nearly 50 and I won a surf board,' his expression changes, 'which I do my ironing on.'

He's not sure if the young are drawn to the role because House is such a maverick or because he doesn't seemed weighed down by political correctness. 'That's appealing to young people, because House is a character who frets against authority and resists being controlled by those who have power over him. And it's appealing to an older generation that has grown impatient with the soft platitudes of modern discourse and political correctness. House demands things be done in the most effective and efficient way possible, and I think audiences really respond to that.'

Young or old he feels that the audience can relate to his human side the more the character progresses. 'He is not Mr Spock,' Laurie says. 'He's is prey to the same weaknesses as anyone else. He may think he's above certain things, and he may think that elements of his behaviour up to this point have been justified. But he also asks himself if he does what he does because he likes it, or because has a weakness for it. He asks, "Am I a weak man?" That's one of the many things he has to confront.'

As the life-changing second series ended, Hugh received a Golden Globe Award for the Best Actor in a Drama Series. It's a side of the business that doesn't sit well with him, but he realises getting awards means more to some people than to others and it comes with the territory. Laurie recalls a personal experience from his childhood. 'The last time I won an award for acting, my parents were in the audience. I had to turn around and I saw their faces as my name was read out. And they smiled at each other, a smile of pride. And that has stayed with me, because to be honest, I didn't give my parents a lot of reasons to be proud. But this was one of them. I was nine years old.'

The night of the award ceremony gave Hugh the opportunity to give the watching public a glimpse of the man behind the fake accent and limp. His acceptance speech brought the house down when he told everyone that he had many people to thank for helping him receive the award and then produced a list which he claimed contained 172 names. Instead of going through them all, he simply picked out three at random and said everyone else could just lump it.

He went on to thank the show's script supervisor and his hair stylist and then his agent, Christian Hodell, before checking the note and adding, 'That's not my handwriting... oh, he's good.'

The place was in an uproar as the laughter filled the room. When it died down, Hugh did put on a serious face to congratulate the main movers and shakers behind the show. He thanked Paul Attanasio, the man behind the original concept; Bryan Singer who, Hugh teased, was a rampant hypochondriac; Katie Jacobs, whose wit and taste has stamped itself in every frame of every show; and of course he ended his speech by recognising David Shore, the main creator, 'Who is one of the finest writers it had been my privilege to say the lines of.' Then he joked that he wished David had been there to help him with the middle of that sentence.

He recognised the rest of the cast and writers, and gave a special mention to his best mate, Stephen Fry, who had travelled from the UK to witness the event and was sitting in the crowd with Hugh's wife, Jo. Last of all he acknowledged his children. 'They're sitting at home, in which case I say to them now, go to bed.'

Disappointedly, that same year he wasn't nominated for an Emmy for his performance as he had been for the series before. Yet, not to be outdone he almost stole the show on the night of the award ceremony with a wonderful spoof appearance as House with Conan O' Brien. Later in the night he popped up yet again, this time speaking French, to present fellow Brit Helen Mirren with an award for Best Actress.

So with a Golden Globe for Best Actor in a TV Series under his belt, the modest star joked that from now on he was definitely going to up his demands while working on set, since he was now an international star. 'I am certainly going to be demanding fresh figs every morning! They must be flown in from Algeria and only Algeria. And I will also bathe my temples in champagne.'

By the time series three was aired, *House* was a phenomenon worldwide, with an estimated 80 million fans watching in 66 different countries. As the viewing figures increased, so apparently did Hugh's salary, which reportedly touched $300k per episode, which is around $7 million per series, making him one of the top earners on the small screen in a land which looks after their TV stars very well indeed. By the show's fifth season, Laurie was earning around $400,000 per episode, making him one of the highest paid actors on network television. Not bad for someone who is happy to wear the label of lazy and says he wanders through life with no plan.

'I'm still reeling. I'm still taking it all in. I've been doing this for 20-odd years and never really been sure that I've been doing the right thing, which I've been in the right place at the right time. It's wonderful to feel at last that maybe I didn't pick the wrong career, that I didn't take a wrong turning, that maybe this is something that I ought to be doing.'

The response from the professionals in the world of medicine, by and large, has been positive, but not all see the show as the way the real world works. 'We may commit terrible solecisms here and there,' says Hugh, who takes criticism seriously. 'Or we make shortcuts that aren't quite believable. The science may be flaky here and there, but it has to be. We have to play fast and loose sometimes just to get the story to work in 42 minutes.'

Leonard is more positive on its affects with the medical profession. 'I've heard from doctors that it's sort of a nice outlet. They watch it and laugh and feel that Hugh's character tends to say all the things they wish they could say.'

One of the challenges for the writers, due to the show's rapid success, was the need for original material and more weird and wonderful diseases. 'We had a bank of unusual ailments that we ran out of around Christmas time on the second series,' Shore joked. 'That was my big worry going into this. Yet there was no need to worry because it proved to be the case of one odd disease down, 99 (or more) to go. I've been shocked how they've been coming, how we're finding more and more unusual stories and unusual things to happen to people. If we can stumble upon a symptom we haven't used before, that's great, because obviously we can't end every act break with a seizure.'

As well as the script development, Hugh was conscious that he needed to continually expand and explore the character, to keep him one step ahead and to ensure he didn't get too boring or predictable. 'I always felt he's on the side of the angels without actually being one.'

Laurie admitted he did experiment with pain killers in order to feel what House was actually going through. Although he only did it in the name of acting, it was an experience he doesn't recommend to anyone else. 'I just wanted to know what that was like. And very pleasant it was, too. I'm aware of having lost half a million brain cells, and I didn't have that many to start with.'

But House's addiction goes beyond just pain killers. 'He's addicted in many ways, not just to pain killers and problem solving. He's addicted to all kinds of patterns of behaviour. He reverts back to being mean and lonely, that's part of his battle and he's not going to one day see the light.'

Shore defends the criticism that the show sometimes receives regarding House's addiction. 'It's not a show about addiction, but you can't throw something like this into the mix and not expect it to be noticed and commented on. There have been references to the amount of his consumption increasing over time. It's becoming less and less useful a tool for dealing with his pain, and it's something we're going to continue to deal with, continue to explore.'

In early 2007, during series four, Hugh won his second Golden Globe Award for Best Actor in a Drama Series, plus he landed the award for Best Actor in a Television Drama from the Screen Actors Guild. The awards kept rolling in and his speeches just kept getting more and more entertaining. His speech after winning his second Golden Globe was typical of Hugh when stripped down to his glorious best. 'I am absolutely speechless. Seriously, I don't have a speech. People are falling all over themselves to send you free shoes and free cuff links and colonic irrigations for two. Nobody ever offers you a free acceptance speech. There just seems to be a gap in the market. I would love to be able to pull out a speech by Dolce & Gabbana.'

The sudden rise in his profile led to appearances on chat shows and to his face on the covers of many magazines, which transformed him from 'Hugh Laurie, middle class bumbling fool' to 'Hugh Laurie, the stubble faced, rock'n'roll, T-shirt wearing sex symbol', with thousands of women swooning over him and many middle-aged men wanting to be him.

'I think he's hot. He's a sex bomb. Let's face it,' says Lisa Edelstein, who portrays House's boss.

'I think the show wouldn't be on the air if we did not have Hugh Laurie in this role. It's a tough character to play and play well,' Shore says. 'To have turned that character into one of the sexiest characters on TV, that is not something I foresaw when I was writing this. I think it's the blue eyes.'

Typically, the married father-of-three is quick to dispel any 'ridiculous' notions of him being anything close to a sex symbol. 'It's utterly absurd. Weird. Deranged. Very amusing. I can't explain it. Even my wife doesn't think I'm sexy, it's a miracle we have children.'

He finds it all quite 'baffling'. 'I hesitate to comment on that, because it's career-ending stuff. I did, however, get a long chain of begging letters from a woman asking if I would go to a hospital in Wyoming or somewhere and visit her mother, who was very unwell, because she watched the show and she would love to meet, etc. etc. and I was thinking, yes, well, but that's not me.' He added, 'The woman wants to meet a fictional character, and that's an unanswerable request.' He knits his fingers together. 'It's so hard to know how to deal with it. You don't want to shatter anyone's illusions, but I'd feel so fraudulent. I might as well dress up as Jesus and do the rounds.' He frowns. 'It was very intrusive, and odd.'

The whole thing makes him feel embarrassed and it's evident in his reactions, although he admits it's the character of House, not him that people see. 'House is a sexy character in his own way. You know, he's that sort of wounded genius. There's a *Beauty and the Beast* element and a bit of the *Phantom of the Opera* thrown in. House is a scarred figure hiding in the upper reaches of the opera house. I can see there's something attractive about that. Women want to fix him. For some reason women find that terribly sexy. He tells the truth, come what may, no matter the consequences. These days that's a bit thrilling. He can unlock secrets, and he isn't afraid to do it no matter what the secrets are.'

However, Hugh's opinion of himself maybe in the minority of one because even the cast believes he's worth the tag of sex symbol. 'But in truth, he is a serious actor. And a sexy guy in real life,' said Jennifer Morrison. 'I think it comes really naturally to him, and obviously he doesn't feel that way. I think it's who he really is, I mean, he's a musician, he's incredibly funny, incredibly smart, incredibly masculine and those are all qualities he brings to the character. But he feels very separate from this identity as a sex symbol. But it's very easy to see how he is one.' She recalls the day she first noticed. 'We were all at a party after the first season ended, and all of a sudden Hugh shows up. He hops off his bike in this tight T-shirt, clean-shaven, with this gorgeous accent, and I'm thinking, "Wow, I forgot that was underneath there."'

Katie Jacobs is also clearly a huge fan. 'What's interesting about the way he photographs, aside from the fact that he photographs sensationally, is that you can't get close enough. The closer you get with the camera, the more his face really comes alive, the more you can see into those eyes and his soul. A lot of actors don't have that; they have the dramatic skills, but that magnetism is something you can't manufacture.'

Again to prove Hugh wrong, or maybe to prove him right, in 2008, Gregory House was voted second sexiest TV doctor ever, behind Dr Doug Ross (George Clooney) from *ER*. He thinks it's nothing short of hilarious to even be mentioned in the same breath as George Clooney. 'George Clooney is very easy on the eye, I'm the ogre on the set.'

The series is now a regular on TV's across the world, and at the time of writing, it was up to series seven with another two already pencilled in. Hugh still has to pinch himself at times to make sure it's not just a dream. 'I've already been doing *House* for a long time. I've got more security than people who work in banks or insurance companies, which is a bit odd. There are these classic statistics in the life of a US show. First you have to nurse it through its infancy, the first six weeks, when it's in the incubator. That's the most dangerous time. And if you make it to two years, you'll probably do six seasons, if not more, unless you fuck up on a grand scale, which we may yet do. But even if people fall out of love with it, there'll be a gradual fading out. Which is actually what one dreads, isn't it?' He shrugs. 'The lingering whimper.'

Although the limp is an integral part of his character, he believes it may also be the thing that forces him from continuing to do the show in years to come because of the pain of contorting his body. 'The show might last to series seven, eight or nine but I don't know if I will, because I'm starting to lose my knees a little bit. It's a lot of hip work. There are things going badly wrong. I need to do yoga.'

Hugh still struggles to acknowledge that the success of the show is as much down to him as anything else. 'I massively question my ability as an actor. I'm aware that what success I have is because I'm playing a fantastic character with brilliant scripts. I'm like a racing driver with the fastest car. That doesn't make me a good driver, but I have a head start.'

He talks with surprise on *House*'s continued success and its ability to continue to attract such huge numbers episode after episode, season after season in such a competitive business with big hungry wolves snapping at its heels. 'It's hard to say if I'm pleased with the show,' he says. 'I don't watch regularly. I avert my eyes when my children have it on. I hate seeing myself, but it's even worse hearing my American accent. I had no idea I sound so retarded, a dull monotone, full of clunking mistakes.'

Whether Hugh watches the show or not, there is no stopping the *House* phenomenon as it rolls on and on, breaking down walls on its remarkable journey. *House* was the most watched television programme in the world in 2008. The show has received several awards, including a People's Choice Award, a Peabody Award, two Golden Globe Awards, and three Primetime Emmy Awards.

For his portrayal of Gregory House, Hugh Laurie has won various awards, including two Golden Globe Awards for Best Actor in a Television Drama Series and a Screen Actors Guild Award for Best Actor from Drama Series. Laurie also earned Primetime Emmy Award nominations in 2005, 2007, 2008 and 2009.

One of the judges of the American Film Institute on the show's 2005 win said. '*House* has redefined the medical television show. No longer a world where an idealised doctor has all the answers or a hospital where gurneys race down the hallways, *House*'s focus is on the pharmacological – and the intellectual demands of being a doctor. The trial-and-error of new medicine skilfully expands the show beyond the format of a classic procedural, and at the show's heart, a brilliant but flawed physician is doling out the prescriptions – a fitting symbol for modern medicine.'

'I'm very fond of House, actually. I love the mixture of light and dark in him, the fact that, at times, he is an eight-year-old child and at others an avenging angel ready to slay the dragons.'

Hugh Laurie

CHAPTER 15

'RIDER AT THE GATES OF DAWN'

One of the advantages of being the hottest and sexiest TV doctor since George Clooney is that when Hugh is not working 16-hour days on set he can indulge in some of his passions, some newly discovered and some which have been with him for a long time.

His love affair with motorcycles dates back to before he can remember. One of the first things he did when the second series of *House* was commissioned, was buy himself his favourite motorbike of all time, a 790cc twin-cylinder Triumph Bonneville.

'I've been riding bikes for more than 30 years now. I started when I was ten riding a two-stroke moped around a field and now my kids are into them. I don't claim to have many skills in life but I do know how to handle a bike.'

Triumph is a British-made bike. The first model rolled off the production line in Coventry in the West Midlands, UK in

1902. With its dark, brooding features, it quickly received cult status as a long line of celebrities strapped their legs around its engine and showed off to the world. James Dean owned a T100, Marlon Brando rode a Thunderbird in *The Wild One*, and Steve McQueen famously lead the entire German army on a wild goose chase astride a T110 in *The Great Escape*.

Hugh's Triumph Bonneville is a replica of a classic bike made in the sixties. At the time it was billed as 'the best motorcycle in the world' when launched in 1959, something Laurie still believes is true today. It got its named after a land-speed record (193mph) was set by a modified Triumph on Bonneville Salt Flats, Utah, a few years before it went into production.

'I couldn't live without it. It's an exhilarating, sensual thing,' he says.

Of course with Hugh's bank balance growing by the day, he could have easily selected a more expensive machine to get around in, and indeed he was tempted to do so for a few minutes. 'I was watching *Biker Build-Off* [a TV series] and there was this Japanese custom bike designer called Shinya Kimura. You could tell within seconds he was a genius. It was $26,000. I thought, "I can't possibly justify that" and then I thought, "Well, why am I doing this job?"' But in the end he didn't buy it. 'No. Something in me says you shouldn't have toys,' he added.

If truth be told he probably could have bought three Triumphs for the price of an average Harley Davidson. 'I wasn't going to ride a Harley Davidson and that's about the only other choice you have in America. It's either something British or American, and I never got into American bikes.

Harleys are slow, expensive, can't corner and don't stop very well. They look like the shop window of Harrods at Christmas.' He wanted a bike not just for show. 'We all have to decide in life, Are we going to remain faithful to a single example or are we going to become collectors? And I'm quite anti-collecting.'

Despite Hugh's long experience with bikes, the notion of their newest, biggest star on a potentially deadly vehicle must have been a major concern for the executives at Fox Network. Although he knew they were more than a little nervous, he's sure they're pretty cool about it, but he laughs when he explains that he keeps telling them that nobody has a greater interest in not falling off than he does. 'Fortunately, I signed the contract before anybody was watching the show, so they couldn't be bothered whether I wiped out or not. I hope it doesn't bother them too much that I drive my motorcycle to work, for instance, and generally enjoy speeding around the hills of LA. But I maintain that no one has a greater interest in me not falling off than I do. I claim supremacy in that area.'

The truth is, he feels safer on a bike than in a car. 'I ride better than I drive because I do it more. And now they've let me do it for 18 months I think it's going to be hard for them to say, "Now the show is doing this well, we value your life. Before we didn't care if you lived or died."'

Yet in the cold light of day, he believes it's not his own driving which is the problem. It's the rest of California he's worried about. 'They have big cars here and they are the most pathetic motorists I have ever come across anywhere in the world, without exception. I went driving with my wife, Jo. We were on the road for 90 minutes and we saw three accidents. The third was a man who'd turned his car over on the roof driving along a dead straight road. How did he manage that? In London you could drive for a year and you probably wouldn't see three accidents.'

At times he says that driving around LA is like being in a video game. 'But unlike many folks at the wheel, I am occupied with getting where I'm going and keeping myself safe. Most people are applying make-up, texting and checking out the beauty in the next car. Here people just cannon into one another almost as a sport. It's just a gigantic pinball machine. I don't think it's America. I think it's limited to Los Angeles, but it makes the ride to work interesting.'

Despite the risk, driving alone in the LA sunshine is a truly wonderful experience that Hugh says he wouldn't swap for the world as he rides majestically to the Fox studios at around 5.30 each morning. 'I travel to work on my bike, so it's jeans, boots and a brown Aero leather jacket that weighs as much as I do. Driving a motorcycle is like flying,' he says. 'All your senses are alive. The greatest thing about riding in Los Angeles is the smell. When I go to work, it's 6 o'clock in the morning. And what they do in the public parks and lawns is they turn the sprinklers on around 3 or 4 in the morning, I guess before it gets hot. So when you go to work at 6 o'clock in the morning, the smell of the trees and plants is just exquisite. My favourite time of day is riding through Los Angeles at the dawn. It's just beautiful.'

Unfortunately, he has had one motorcycle crash since living in LA, but only a minor one, which actually left him with five stitches in his eyebrow. 'It was during the pilot, so no one knew who House was. It happened on a Friday and I was back at work on Monday, so it didn't hold us up.'

It wasn't until the second series that the audience got to witness House on a motorcycle, along with a convenient slot along the side to place his cane in like a gunslinger's holster. 'People always ask me how I cope with the fact that House rides a motorbike. So it usually comes as a surprise when I tell them that I've been riding motorcycles since I was 12 years old. I still ride everyday so I have it pretty much down by now. Motorbikes are my daily transport both in England as well as LA. The producers of *House* knew that when I signed to do the show and the writer who introduced the motorcycle is also a rider. So I suppose you could say it's a two-wheel bonding type of thing.'

Despite his character's bad leg, the Honda Repsol replica became a semi-regular part of House's routine. Hugh of course would have preferred a Triumph but it wouldn't have fitted the image of the TV doctor. 'It was the show's idea to have House ride a Honda,' he said. 'House is tight with money, and the implication is that he picked up that Honda cheap. If House were to end up on a Triumph, it'd have to be because he won it in a poker game. The Honda, that's a sports bike,' he adds. 'That's a sort of flat-out, as fast as you can go, "Rider at the Gates of Dawn" kind of a bike. A speed demon.' Whereas Laurie reckons the Triumph Bonneville is much more sedate and much more practical. 'And I really don't use it for entertainment. I use it to get to work. I use it to commute. I can get through traffic, and I can park it easily, and it's cheap to run,' he says. 'And everyone should ride a Triumph!' He is always willing to try and persuade people to buy British!

If driving a motorbike wasn't enough to give the studio sleepless nights, he also fell in love with another dangerous pastime: the art of boxing. He had originally been an avid jogger but a low boredom threshold caused him to search out some other activity to keep him trim. 'Jogging is incredibly tedious,' he says. 'I know it has benefits, and I feel bad when I don't do it, but I don't feel that great when I do do it!'

Then he got introduced to boxing, and now spars with, or gets beaten badly by, an instructor a few times a week. 'Boxing is fascinating. It's good for the soul to be made to feel clumsy. I swank around during the week thinking I'm a big cheese, but you don't feel like that when you're in the ring with a chap who knows what he's doing. It's ritual humiliation. I'm going to be slugged about and probably killed, but I love it and have to do something to keep fit, and it's also good for the heart.'

Hugh confesses to being hopeless at boxing but can't get enough of the tough activity. 'I absolutely love it. Well, I sort of love it. But it's love mixed with fear. Not fear of physical harm, because unless you do it repeatedly and get hit in the head a lot, you'll survive. It's more the fear of being humiliated, which sort of messes with your perceptions of, I suppose, maleness. To question your maleness is a very intense experience. But there's something else. When I'm making a television show, eight months go by just like that. It's a wonderful thing to have a completely opposite experience, which is to get into the ring for three minutes and have time essentially stop. You cannot believe how long three minutes is until you've spent time in a boxing ring. If we could live our lives as intensely as one does in those three minutes, it would be like living for 10,000 years. I love that feeling.'

Although a novice, he quotes that it is the hardest thing he's ever done, but well worth all the effort and sweat. 'To throw a good punch is as hard as hitting a good forehand or a good golf shot. But those guys hitting good forehands and golf shots don't have someone hitting them in the face while they're doing it, which, I can tell you, throws you off your game a bit.'

He trains at a Hollywood gym and he reckons it has something to do with 'the desire to live intensely'. He now appreciates how hard the sport is and frequently goes to watch the real professionals in the ring, often taking his son along with him. 'I don't know if I'm looking to affirm masculinity, but there is something going on there, a feeling of men testing themselves, and when the test is over a weirdly gentle atmosphere and a feeling of comradeship.'

Yet he has no desire to do it himself professionally. 'I'm not even sure I could throw a punch in an actual boxing match. I sparred last week. One of the interesting things about sparring, about boxing, is discovering the barrier you have in your own mind to trying to hit someone. You've got all the problems of trying to stop him from hitting you and various technical things to deal with. But there comes a point when you miss a chance to hit someone because you hesitated, because it is in one's nature, or in one's culture, not to punch someone. Boxing is what it is, and you have to get over that. The most interesting aspect of boxing is the sheer science of it. To people who haven't had much experience, it looks like two guys just flailing around in a ring. It's far from that.'

Hugh knows his limitations and the limits his career has placed on his boxing enthusiasm. With his face being an important element to his fortune, he's forced to practise what he calls 'a kind of girlie boxing'. Nevertheless, he likes the way the exercise clears his head, unless of course he's getting whacked by someone, and how it offsets his work. Doing ten months as House seems to fly, but three minutes in the ring, on the other hand, sometimes seem like eternity. He jokes that his favourite opponent would be little children. 'That would heighten my chances of winning considerably. They should be five years of age at the most.'

Maybe in the future House will be seen donning boxing gloves, or, more likely, Hugh will be seen sparring with someone in the name of charity.

One of Hugh's other greatest passions has already become a regular addition to the series. Hugh often describes himself as 'a frustrated musician', while adding that music is the one place where he can really lose himself. 'I can sit at my piano for what seems like five minutes, but when I look at the clock it's three in the morning.'

Music plays a large part in his family's life, too. He plays guitar and piano while his two boys play saxophone and drums and his daughter fills in on the clarinet. It is truly a very musical family.

In fact, Laurie's secret dream is to make music and play in a hotel jazz band with two other mates when he hangs up his acting boots. He jokes, or maybe not, that the group would be called the Hugh Laurie Five, even though there would only be three musicians. 'I am going to form a jazz trio along the lines of a Ramsey Lewis or Herbie Hancock kind of thing. I'm gonna find some regular gigs, and we'll play a very groovy set. If girls in tight-fitting cocktail dresses want to drape themselves over the piano, that's fine, but the music's the thing. That's one of the few things I'm sure about, I know, I just know, that will make me immensely happy.'

In his past, around the time of the *Bit of Fry and Laurie* period, he did play keyboards in a soul/R&B band with Lenny Henry and Ben Elton's wife Sophie; it also included Adrian Edmondson of *The Young Ones* for a short while until he quit due to musical differences. They were called Poor White Trash and the Little Big Horns.

At the time it brought a lot of positive reaction among the press and his peers. 'It was a terrible midlife crisis. Instead of wearing ponytails and sleeping with my secretary, not that I have a secretary to sleep with, I was singing blues.'

He had such a laugh being a fake rock'n'roll star that he was quoted saying that 'he would have to start to go out with Patsy Kensit.' He went on to explain how wild the after-show parties were. 'Occasionally, after a show, we go a bit mad and tread a biscuit into the hotel carpet!'

Yet, it was more than just a hobby or big joke to the members of the band. They took it serious and played some big gigs. Poor White Trash and the Little Big Horns backed up Lenny on the *Comic Relief* broadcast in March 1997. The band further raised its profile by playing two dates at the Edinburgh Festival Fringe in August 1997, to enthusiastic crowds.

Lenny Henry described Poor White Trash in a beeb.com chat in 1998: 'I'm in a band called Poor White Trash and the Little Big Horns. We do gigs for friends and for colleagues. On the rare occasion when we've done proper gigs it's been good but not quite the same, so we tend to do them for our mates really. I'm the lead singer, Hugh Laurie's the keyboard player;

we've got the Level 42 horn section, Then Jericho's programmer, The Spice Girls' drummer and two brilliant backing singers. And we're funky and we're live and we sweat and people dance and go mad. But it's just a hobby. It's a bit late for me to become a pop star now...we're a hard-working soul band and we do well.'

They thrashed out some classic hits such as 'Soul Man' and 'Mustang Sally'. Lenny confessed that his wife, comedienne Dawn French, thought it was all one big joke. 'The missus says it's a mid-life crisis waiting to happen, but I love singing and I wanted to do something groovy,' he added. 'Every so often we get together, do R&B covers, eat sandwiches, drink beer and have a laugh.'

More recently, while settling in the States, Hugh played with the Los Angeles charity group Band from TV. The Band was formed when actor Greg Grunberg realised that after playing a gig at the House of Blues with a host of celebrities it generated an enormous amount of interest. He saw a chance to play fundraisers for charity with other musical actors. So, when he got to star on an episode of *House*, he quickly asked Hugh Laurie if he would be interested in playing in his group.

'My oldest son has epilepsy,' explained Greg, 'and I saw this band as a wonderful vehicle for helping raise money for the National Epilepsy Foundation. Having band mates who also happen to be in some of the most popular shows on television creates an amazing opportunity to really reach out to our fans to help support these wonderful causes.'

What started out as a love for music and simply having fun jamming with buddies, led Greg Grunberg and his star friends to play their own brand of rock and roll for charity to packed venues. The group made its introduction at the 58th yearly Primetime Emmy Awards in 2006.

The Band From TV line-up includes a powerhouse of well-known and acclaimed actors including, Greg (drums), a veteran of shows such as *Alias* and starring in the NBC hit *Heroes*; James Denton (guitar), currently starring in the ABC hit *Desperate Housewives*; Bob Guiney (vocals) who appeared on game show *The Bachelor* and is currently seen on TLC's *Date My House*; Jesse Spencer (violin), Hugh's co-star in *House*; Adrian Pasdar, from *Heroes* and *Desperate Housewives*; Scott Grimes from *American Dad!* and *ER*; and rounding off the band are accomplished musicians Chris Kelley, Barry Sarna, Jon Sarna, Chris Mostert and child-star turned bass player Brad Savage.

While the members are all talented actors, the band is truly about celebrating music, living the rock and roll fantasy and having fun, while bringing classic rock and roll music to life and raising money. 'Professional musicians need to rehearse a lot and amateur musicians need to rehearse an awful lot more,' Hugh says. 'I haven't had enough time of late to be even an amateur and I began to hate the feeling of getting to the end of a song and only then realising what the song was and what key it should be played in. That's no way to carry on.'

The Band covered songs like the Stones' hit 'You Can't Always Get What You Want' for the *House MD* Master Television Soundtrack, and they frequently play charity events to profit assorted causes. They released a record album entitled *Hoggin' All the Covers* in 2007.

'What I feel like, I suppose, is a jack-of-all-trades, master of none. I've always felt like I could turn my hand to a lot of things but never excel at any of them. I do play the piano a bit, but I wish I could play it like Dr John or Henry Butler. I act, but I wish I could act like Al Pacino. I do a bit of all these things. I'm just trying to dazzle you with quantity. I can't do anything well enough, so I'll do many things and hope that the quantity distracts you from the deficiencies. Maybe that's the plan.'

'I fear happiness because I don't know what follows. To say "I've accomplished something, or I look around and I see that my life pleases me," that would feel like a kind of death.'

Hugh Laurie

CHAPTER 16

'LIFE OUTSIDE OF
THIS BUBBLE'

Like most things in life, success often comes at a cost. For Hugh, that cost was living alone in LA while the people he loved most dearly were on the other side of the world.

Since the early series, he was faced with the major dilemma of whether or not he should uproot his wife, Jo, daughter Rebecca Augusta Laurie, sons Charles 'Charlie' Archibald Laurie and William 'Bill' Albert Laurie, and bring them closer to him.

Although he claims that he is, Hugh is anything but stupid and is well aware that the business he finds himself in can be a notoriously fickle place at the best of times; a business that is willing to brush careers aside in an instant in pursuit of higher ratings. 'I always worry. I'm not religious or superstitious, but I have this vague feeling that the moment I'm comfortable with my place in the world there'll be retribution. That's one reason I didn't want my family to live here. The moment we put down roots the whole thing will be called off.'

So as the first series hit production, he and his family agreed to pretend it was just another assignment for the star and wherever possible see each other, whether it meant Hugh flying home or the whole clan trundling over to LA when he wasn't filming.

For most of that time, while other cast members were signing leases on big houses, Hugh lived in a hotel. He believed they were all mad because in his mind, in a few months it was all going to fall apart. He literally lived out of his suitcase, while waiting for someone to the knock on his door to inform him it was all over. But that knock never came.

'It's very hard, indeed,' he said. 'We're just resigned to doing a lot of travelling. I get back when I can, and they come over here when they can. But it is tough. You know, if this had happened ten years ago when my kids were small, it would have been very easy, maybe, to just take them out of school and put them in school here. But they're teenagers, and they've got their own lives, and it's tough on them to drag them out and go, "Come, build a new life with me, and I'll see you one hour a week anyway." So even when they come here, I don't see them that much.'

Yet the longer the show went on, the more disheartened and exhausted he became when faced with the long transcontinental flight. 'The trip seems to get longer,' he said. 'I used to look forward to a couple of movies. Now, as soon as I get on the plane I get impatient. It is a feral distance.'

Like any good father who finds himself away from his family for such a large amount of time, he knows he is missing his kids growing up. 'My eldest son was one size when I left, and he's probably a cabinet minister now,' he jokes.

But neither the busy schedule nor the distance stopped them from talking on a daily basis, or at the very least a couple of times a week mainly by phone or internet from his West Hollywood apartment. It was good for Hugh to speak in his native tongue before he slipped comfortably back into his American accent and trotted off to work.

'It is hard being away from my family and being in a strange city and living out of a suitcase. It is rough but that's the gypsy nature of what I do. It's remote parenting and it's very tricky. They're teenagers now so they're entering that interesting phase. We talk every day and I've got a little video camera so we can see each other when we talk, and I tell them to eat their broccoli and go to bed early and they pay no attention. They come out here whenever they can and I go out there. We just have to make the best of it.'

Co-star Robert Sean Leonard, who plays Dr Wilson, finds sympathy for his friend's predicament. 'He's got a family thousands of miles away and he's here pretending to be an American. This show is all he has. It's lonely. Every time I see him, I don't know how he does it. His character is so self-destructive that I worry for him, not just that he won't find happiness, but that he might actually do physical harm to himself.'

Of course with the money he earns, he could have easily, and maybe selfishly, just picked them all up and transported them all over. Yet he knows it's not as simple as that and he has had to consider what is best for them. They would be leaving friends and family to come and be with a father that worked 16-hour days.

They realise that it really wouldn't be much different than living thousands of miles apart as they wouldn't see each for more than an hour or so a week. 'They could move here, but the kids would have to go to new schools, and my wife wouldn't know anyone, and none of them would see me anyway. I'm always on the set. I wasn't prepared for this at all, but I don't really have a life outside of this bubble. I'm here from first thing in the morning until last thing at night. We can finish filming between midnight and 4am. Then I'm straight back to bed. It's not really a life, actually, it's a bit like being on an oil rig. I've not had one second of Hollywood life. I haven't even seen a Jacuzzi.'

In such a tough and often lonely business, he often admires those actors in similar situations who stick with it for a long time. 'I'm ready to drop, just bone-weary, although it's a great bunch of people and terrific fun to do.'

It's perhaps these frustrations which have led to reports of Hugh looking miserable and despondent on set, despite the acclaim and awards. It could be worse he says, but he's lucky Jo, his wife, is so grounded and takes on the fatherly duties as well as everything else to ensure the family functions as normally and as smoothly as possible. Hugh is always willing to balance his situation up against others less fortunate than himself, which can often put it all in prescriptive.

'I once met a guy who worked on a nuclear submarine. He had to check a box on a piece of paper saying whether he wanted to be informed in the event that something horrible happened back home because if something horrible did happen, he wasn't getting off that sub. Something did happen to a friend of his and he didn't hear about it until they returned to land. At least I don't have to make that choice. I know if something happens, I can always fly home.'

However, he still knows that without his family by his side, it's easy to sink back into a shell and cover up in self-pity. 'Without them near, I do go quite insane, probably three times a week,' he says. 'It can show itself in all kinds of ways. I mean, who else do you know, who can catch a ball on the top of a cane? I worry about parenting at a distance, but my children are being so generous about it. Of course it might be because they're English and they won't reveal their psychological damage until their late 40s.'

Inevitably, as the show continued on its extended and lucrative run, it was only a matter of time, even for someone as pessimistic as Laurie, to realise something more permanent needed to be done house-wise. So after the cushion of several more series' being promised, he finally decided to stop 'padding around the Chateau Marmont like a ghost', as described by Shore, and he get himself a house in the Hollywood Hills.

The words seem to tumble out of his mouth rather than flow freely as he explains. 'I've put down, not quite roots but more like a flowerpot. My family still lives in London, but I finally had to accept that *House* has some sort of permanence. I was so convinced in the first few years that it was never going to last, because nothing does. Simply statistically, the odds are very much against it in television. But here we are.'

He's not convinced that Los Angeles is a place ever to be thought of as home. 'No one calls it that, Americans or otherwise. It's a place you go to pan for gold, to "realise a project" or to make money, but no one envisages dying there. Well, no one does. It's actually against the law, I think.'

On saying that, the man who was brought up as a Presbyterian in a place where rain and cold and slate-grey brooding skies was the order of the day, admits he does like LA, even if at times he feels like he's on safari looking at a range of exotic animals. 'LA runs on optimism, enthusiasm and flattery. I think you can go a little bit crazy. I've heard people say there's a limit to the number of years you can stay in this city without going slightly mad. It's just too damn sunny in every dimension, weather-wise, socially and professionally.'

Such stark contrast to the cold, damp environment in which he thought he would live out his days, pulling on slightly damp Fair Isle sweaters. 'I do actually like Los Angeles. Partly because I was told I wouldn't. It's partly to do with what people tell you to expect. People said, "Los Angeles is the most terrible place of all. You'll go crazy. You won't last a month. You'll be going out of your mind, it's so superficial. It has a peculiar and powerful reputation, even for Americans. It's a mad place of cocaine, Jacuzzis, flashbulbs and greed." But I'm surprised how ordinary, in a good sense, LA is. Ordinary as in decent, hardworking and functional actually.'

He find himself attracted to the energy and vivacity of the place and of Americans themselves, but he is more than happy to share his thoughts that LA looks like a giant petrol station when compared to the rest of the world.

Of course he misses home, especially the quirkiness of Britain, with its weather and dark buildings, and also its cruelty. 'They're very harsh people, the British. Hard to impress, very tough on each other, but I rather like that. It's not that the British are more honest, you're just under no illusion with them.'

This probably bears itself out with the show *House*. While it gets bigger and bigger around the globe, strangely, or some would say predictably, the series isn't that big a deal in the UK. Hugh reckons it could be down to the British being a nation of Professor Higginses, who find any sort of linguistic affectation drives them absolutely mad.

'It's a long way from *Blackadder*,' he acknowledges, 'which is maybe why the show hasn't become as big in Britain as it has in other places. People still think I'm putting on airs and so it's hard for them to take in.' He believes there's a sense of treachery felt by the British public for any actor who goes abroad to ply his or her trade. In fact, it's not just people in the acting profession; sports stars like footballer David Beckham have also felt the same isolation over the years.

'It's rather frowned upon. There were two beacons on that front, Peter Cook and Dudley Moore. Both were fantastically talented, but Peter stayed in London and Dudley left. Because he left and because he lived in glorious California, Moore was widely assumed to have made a deal with the devil that involved beautiful blonde women and beaches and sunshine and Ferraris. Peter maintained the slightly drizzly temperament we revere in England. Moore was perceived as a traitor.'

Hugh did return to the United Kingdom to meet up with the rest of the family to enjoy a very special day on 23 May 2007, when the 47-year-old star attended a ceremony at Buckingham Palace, where he was made an Officer of the Order of the British Empire (OBE) for his services to drama by Queen Elizabeth II. The award came as a shock and completely out of the blue and his only regret was that his parents weren't there to see it. Hugh's children were delighted and it went a long way in ensuring he achieved one of his principal goals in life of trying to avoid embarrassing them.

As expected for a star like Laurie, the question as to whether he would encourage his kids to enter the world of showbiz often comes up (normally straight after the question 'Are you still depressed?'). He typically replies that he wouldn't encourage them, but they have already dipped their toe in the pool of entertainment. 'They like drama classes at the moment, although I think that's mainly because it's not maths,' he says. Charlie had a cameo in *A Bit of Fry and Laurie* during his infancy in the last sketch of the episode entitled 'Special Squad', as baby William, whom Stephen and Hugh begin to interrogate about 'what he's done with the stuff', calling him a scumbag and telling him that he's been a very naughty boy, while Rebecca had a role in the film *Wit* as five-year-old Vivian Bearing. 'My youngest son, Bill, auditioned for one of the *Harry Potter* films but, at ten, he was too young for the intended role. I have to admit I was relieved it didn't go any further,' he added.

From an early age, he has tried to instil a love of sport in all of his children and he would love his sons to become professional cricketers so he can sit back and watch them play all day. 'I try and console my children when they have not been successful, and I am thrilled when they are,' he says. 'They have no competitive ethos in them.' Laurie is, however, a vocal supporter from the sidelines when his son is playing rugby. 'But I have never gotten to a point where I have threatened a referee.'

He is more than quick to point out that so far his three children have only brought him delight, and are his pride and joy. 'Maybe the distance is an advantage. My wife probably has to bear more fights with them than I do.' Although on the matter of raising his only daughter he says, 'Girls are complicated. The instruction manual that comes with girls is 800 pages, with chapters 14, 19, 26 and 32 missing, and it's badly translated, hard to figure out. Our daughter Rebecca is still relatively young, so maybe there are things yet to come. Girls are supposedly more difficult than boys. By and large we men are rather simple.'

Despite his long hours as House, Hugh has been able to find a little time to star in a few movies. *Street Kings* (originally titled *The Night Watchman*) is a 2008 action-crime film, directed by David Ayer, starring Keanu Reeves as Detective Tom Ludlow, Forest Whitaker as Captain Jack Wander and Hugh Laurie as Captain James Biggs.

It's a movie about a veteran LAPD cop whose life changes after his wife dies, and finds him questioning his fellow officers and in turn the entire police culture. James Ellroy wrote the screenplay after getting inspired by the OJ Simpson trial. Initially, Spike Lee was up for directing the film for a 2005 release but dropped out. Then Oliver Stone was in talks to direct it, which he later denied. However, *Training Day* screenwriter David Ayer took over the project and made a success of it – the film grossed an estimated $62 million in total worldwide sales.

More recently, Hugh was asked to do the voiceover in one of the biggest 3-D animation films made by Dream Works Animation in 2009, *Monsters vs Aliens*. Laurie, who had previously voiced a pigeon in the British animation film *Valiant*, played the part of a cockroach. 'I can imagine the scenario,' he says. "'We have a cockroach. Who are we going to get to play it? I've got it! Hugh Laurie.'"

Other featured voices were Reese Witherspoon, Seth Rogen, Will Arnett, Rainn Wilson, Kiefer Sutherland, Stephen Colbert and Paul Rudd.

The story starts when a meteorite from outer space hits a young California woman named Susan Murphy (Witherspoon), turning her into a giant monster. The government kidnaps her and takes her to a top secret government compound where she meets up with 'other' monsters who have been rounded up over the years. When Earth is threatened by attack from nasty aliens, the motley crew of Monsters are called into action to help save the world from imminent destruction.

Hugh plays one of the monsters, Dr Cockroach, Ph.D, a brilliant but mad scientist who, after an experiment goes wrong, accidentally finds himself with a giant cockroach's head and the ability to climb up walls. Hugh's insect character helps Susan learn more about her condition while in captivity.

The film, which was said to have taken approximately 46 million computer hours to make, eight times as many as the original *Shrek*, was scheduled for a May 2009 release, but the release date was moved to March in the same year to avoid competition with James Cameron's *Avatar*.

On its opening weekend, the film opened at number one, grossing $59 million before going on to become the third highest-grossing animated film of 2009, with a total of $383 million against an estimated budget $175 million dollars to develop it. In 2010, the film was nominated for four Annie Awards (which are presented by the International Animated Film Society and are regarded as Animation's highest honour), including Voice Acting in a Feature Production for Hugh Laurie.

As *House* climbs slowly towards the holy grail of 100 episodes on American television, the star also claims that playing House has gone a long way to curing him of his depression, although he has mentioned it's a part of his life that keeps surfacing out of the mist. It's become an anchor around his neck, weighing him down as journalists bring it up at every opportunity. 'I wish I'd kept my mouth shut about that,' Laurie says. 'That's an example of me throwing open the doors and trusting, and then coming downstairs and finding the TV is gone. Now an undue weight has been given to this aspect of my life.' He doesn't want to be known as the guy who has nothing else to talk about except how miserable he is all of the time, because he knows he is incredibly fortunate and blessed to be in the situation in which he finds himself. 'I remember watching Mel Gibson on some show once, and he was being asked about his belief in the afterlife. Gibson said, "Well, I can't believe this is all there is." And I thought, "Wait a minute. You're Mel Gibson. You have millions of dollars. You're a great-looking chap with every conceivable blessing that could be bestowed upon a man. And that's not good enough?" So you can see why I'm hesitant to talk about any trivial pain I have. I find myself going, "Oh, for God's sake, Hugh. Pull yourself together."'

Again, Leonard, who is aware of the demons his co-star's been fighting with for most of his life, comes to his defence.

'You don't play a character like that with any kind of success unless you have some deep waters. A happy person acting unhappy is unbearable to watch. He's not misery on the set; he's actually very quiet and easygoing. But it's that Peter Cook thing, misery turned into brilliance.'

The lonely lifestyle and long hours does get him down on times but would probably get most sane of people down. Hugh knows he's not the happiest person who has ever walked the planet, but the older he gets the more he tries to change, even if it means at least making the people's day around him a little easier. 'If I can't make my own any better, I try to be more cheerful or pretend to be more cheerful. I'll settle for pretend at the moment.'

He still feels it necessary to go and talk to his shrink for an hour once a week. It's a way of dealing with the stress of being on a hit show and the stress of knowing his family are thousands of miles away. 'I'd been doing this job over there for a while, and I hate to use the word stressful. It's not stressful like being in Baghdad – but it got to me, and continues to do so from time to time in a big way. But things are only stressful if you care about them. Marcus Aurelius, I think it was who said, "If you are distressed by anything external, the pain is not due to the thing itself, but to your own estimate of it and this you have the power to revoke at any moment."'

Of course for someone like Hugh, who doesn't really like the spotlight, it's all the trappings that come with fame that may one day tip him back over the edge. Fame means paparazzi following his every move, photographers behind every tree looking for a snap or gossip. 'It used to be the case that the only people who paid any attention to me were those who liked what I did,' he says. 'Now I get noticed by people who don't care whether I live or die, probably want me to die. That takes a bit of getting used to.'

And in his case it doesn't get any better, as he currently finds himself right on top of the fame-mountain – a recent poll named Laurie in the top five favourite television personalities in the US, up there with Oprah and Jay Leno. 'That's an exaggeration. I am being very handsomely paid, though. My ship has come in and I'll be forever grateful.' It makes him feel guilty, and question the whole idea of being a celebrity. 'It's absolutely preposterous. Entertainment seems to be inflating.' It's not celebrities he admires, he says, but 'those blokes in Fair Isle sweaters with pencils behind their ears who knew how to design mechanical things better than anybody else in the world.'

Now, years after first stepping in the shoes of Doctor Gregory House, Hugh's unsure how long he can continue to pull it off or how long the show will go on for. He keeps thinking of the self-destructive element of House, like a guy who is standing out on the window ledge before making a decision. 'You either have to jump or get back into the window. You can't stand there for 15 years because the audience will be like, "Oh, jump! Come on." It just gets too frustrating.'

Who knows how Hugh would feel if it all finished tomorrow? He may be delighted because he stills feels as though he's got so much more to do. Even as he passes the half-century mark in his life, he fears he's still trying to work out who he is and what profession he should be doing. He's aware that *House* gave him a shot, the biggest shot in his life, a shot where many British actors have tried but failed. And he took his opportunity with both hands.

Many people would be more than happy with what he's achieved, but his mind isn't wired the same way and he struggles with fame, struggles with self-deprecation, and is always hyper-critical of himself as he sees the glass half empty instead of the other way around. He recalls the day on set when he experienced his first ever earthquake. 'We were shooting, the camera was rolling, and everything started to sway. The lamps started to move. I loved it. I loved it. It passed quickly, and we were back to work. But let's say that had been, you know, the big one, if that were the end. I can't tell you how many things I would regret not having done. The list would have a billion things on it.'

Maybe it's just a mid-life crisis the same as most men go through. 'I had ambitions of opening the batting for England, climbing Kilimanjaro. I assumed there was plenty of time, but now the clocks have gone forward and I'm late, stuck because all my fantasies were based on the achievements of younger men like David Gower. I have no older role models. I don't want to become home secretary or conduct the Philharmonic. Who would I be now as an actor, father, husband, writer? I don't know. And that's tragic. This realisation should have happened when I was 35, but being rather dim I didn't perceive it until six months ago.'

He is becoming more vocal these days about the fact that finding joy is absolutely the essential thing for him as a person who has reached this point in his life. It has become his obsession as he tries his best to fight against his fear of happiness. 'Fear is probably my only obstacle to it right now. I have a very good life. I am fortunate in so many ways. Now the secret is simply to delight in every breath and every step.'

Everything he has done, he's done well, and he has made it look so easy. Even though he's the last to admit to it, he has proved he has got his father's drive and the grit determination to succeed with most things thrown at him. Underneath all of his humorous self-putdowns, the tests and the challenges he's faced look like they have spurred him on. His sporting achievements go a long way in telling that story, as does the hours and hours of practice he must have endured in his life to become an accomplished musician – not forgetting the small matter of him becoming a published author.

Does any of it make him really happy, that's the question? He is now a phenomenon, a man who was part of a glorious period in British comedy, a best-selling author, an accomplished musician, a sportsman, family man, and critically acclaimed actor. Most people would have to live five lifetimes to get anywhere close to achieving what Hugh Laurie as achieved.

His attitude and the way he looks at life is no different now from what it was in the early days – a humorous, and very likable man with something of a dark side. This was the man who said, 'If I don't have a stone in my shoe, I'll put one in there.' But now, as he gets older, that dark side appears to be getting marginally a little brighter.

'I still amble along and I don't have answers. I never have had. In fact, that would be my epitaph. I just don't know. Because, let's face it, who does? Either that or, "Here lies Hugh Laurie. He always cleaned up after himself."'

'It would start with a full English breakfast, then I'd go to a motorcycle shop to test ride their newest, shiniest, stupidest bike. I'd go to Prague and, en route, have lunch in a motorway café, eaten outside so I can hear the tick, tick of hot metal. Then I'd come home and have a Chinese dinner with the wife and our friends, playing the piano brilliantly with a group of musicians.'

Hugh Laurie

INTERESTING FACTS

**Famous Alumni of Hugh's Alma Mater,
Selwyn College Cambridge:**

Clive Anderson, 1952–, Former barrister, comedian
and television presenter
Richard Budgett, 1959–, Olympic rowing gold medallist
Ralph Chubb, 1892–1960, Poet and printer
Graham Connah, Archaeologist
Alvin Robert Cornelius, 1903–1991, Chief Justice
of the Supreme Court of Pakistan
Rt Hon John Selwyn Gummer, 1939–, British politician
Richard Harries, 1936–, Former Bishop of Oxford
and life peer
Robert Harris, 1957–, Author
Tom Hollander, 1967–, Actor

Karl Hudson-Phillips QC, 1933–, Former judge of the
International Criminal Court

Angus Maddison, 1926–2010, Economist

Simon Hughes, 1951–, Politician

Grayston 'Bill' Ives, 1948–, Composer

Lionel Charles Knights, 1906–1997, Literary critic

Hugh Laurie, 1959–, Comedian and actor

Ran Laurie, 1915–1998, Olympic rowing champion
and gold medallist

Ivan Lloyd-Phillips, 1910–1984, Civil servant

Sir Richard May, 1938–2004, Judge

David Miller, 1946–, Political theorist

Barry Morgan, 1947–, Archbishop of Wales

Malcolm Muggeridge, 1903–1990, Author and journalist

Robert Newman, 1964–, Comedian and author

Nigel Newton, 1955–, Founder of Bloomsbury Publishing

Sir Edwin Nixon, 1925–2008, Managing director
of IBM (UK)

Mario Petrucci, 1958–, Poet, essayist and critic

John Sentamu, 1949–, Archbishop of York

Sir Peter Singer, 1944–, Judge

Adrian Smith, 1957–, Statistician

Sir Peter Smith, 1952–, Judge

Wes Streeting, 1983–, President of the National Union
of Students

Graham Stuart, 1962–, Politician

Nick Tanner, Actor

David KR Thomson, 1957–, Businessman and member
of Canada's wealthiest family

APPENDIX

Famous members of Cambridge Footlights:

Many prominent figures in the world of entertainment and the arts began their careers in Footlights. They include:

Douglas Adams, 1952–2001, Writer

Clive Anderson, 1952–, Comedian, television presenter

David Armand, 1977–, Comedian, actor

Alexander Armstrong, 1970–, Comedian

Pete Atkin, 1945–, Singer-songwriter

Richard Ayoade, 1977–, Comedian, actor

David Baddiel, 1964–, Comedian, novelist, television presenter

Morwenna Banks, 1964–, Comedian and actor

Humphrey Barclay, 1941–, Comedy executive, producer

Tom Basden, 1981–, Actor, comedy writer, singer-songwriter

Cecil Beaton, 1904–1980, Photographer

Simon Bird, 1984–, Actor, Comedian

Leslie Bricusse, 1931–, Lyricist, composer

Eleanor Bron, 1938–, Actress, writer

Tim Brooke-Taylor, 1940–, Comedy writer and performer, lawyer

Robert Buckman, 1948–, Comedian, writer, physician, television presenter, columnist

Tony Buffery, Psychologist

Jon Canter, Script-writer

Graham Chapman, 1941–1989, Comedian, actor, writer, physician

John Cleese, 1939–, Comedian, actor, writer

Olivia Colman, 1974–, Comedian, actor

Peter Cook, 1937–1995, Comedian, writer, satirist

Joe Craig, 1980–, Novelist, musician

Hugh Dennis, 1962–, Comedian, actor, writer, voice-over artist

Jimmy Edwards, 1920–1988, Radio and television comedy actor

Alan Fleming-Baird, 1972–, Composer

David Frost, 1939–, Television presenter, journalist

Stephen Fry, 1957–, Comedian, writer, actor, novelist

Graeme Garden, 1943–, Comedy writer and performer, physician, illustrator

Mel Giedroyc, 1968–, Actor, writer, television presenter

Germaine Greer, 1939–, Writer, broadcaster, academic

Nick Hancock, 1962–, Actor, comedian, television presenter

Norman Hartnell, 1901–1979, Fashion designer

David Hatch, 1939–2007, Management and production at the BBC

Natalie Haynes, 1974–, Comedian, writer

Tony Hendra, 1941–, Satirist, writer

Kit Hesketh-Harvey, 1957–, Comic performer, scriptwriter

Tom Hollander, 1967–, Actor

Matthew Holness, Comedian

Claude Hulbert, 1900–1964, Comic actor

Jack Hulbert, 1892–1978, Actor

Eric Idle, 1943–, Comedian, actor, writer, songwriter

Clive James, 1939–, Writer, poet, critic, TV presenter

Simon Jones, 1950–, Actor

Jo Kendall, Actor

Tim Key, 1976–, Comedian, actor, poet

Ian Lang, 1940–, Former politician, life peer

Hugh Laurie, 1959–, Comedian, actor, writer, novelist

Jonathan Lynn, 1943–, Comedy writer, actor, director

Miriam Margolyes, 1941–, Actor

Dan Mazer, 1971–, Comedian, producer, screenwriter

Kevin McCloud, 1959–, Writer, designer, television presenter

Rory McGrath, 1956–, Comedian

Ben Miller, 1966–, Comedian, director, actor

Jonathan Miller, 1934–, Neurologist, theatre and
   opera director, humorist, sculptor

David Mitchell, 1974–, Comedian, actor, writer

Lucy Montgomery, 1975–, Comedian, actor, writer

Neil Mullarkey, Comedian, actor, writer

Jimmy Mulville, 1955–, Comedian, comedy writer,
   television presenter and producer

Simon Munnery, Comedian

Richard Murdoch, 1907–1990, Radio, film and
   television performer

Bill Oddie, 1941–, Comedy writer and performer,
   musician, ornithologist, television presenter

John Oliver, 1977–, Comedian, comedy writer,
   television personality

Sue Perkins, 1969–, Actress, comedian, writer,
   television presenter

Steve Punt, 1962–, Comedian, actor, writer

Jan Ravens, 1958–, Actor, impressionist

Griff Rhys Jones, 1953–, Comedian, actor, writer,
   television presenter

Blake Ritson, 1980–, Actor, director, writer

Charles Shaughnessy, 1955–, Actor, television writer

Julian Slade, 1930–2006, Writer of musical theatre

Tony Slattery, 1959–, Comedian, actor

Dan Stevens, 1982–, Actor
William Sutcliffe, 1971–, Novelist
Joe Thomas, 1985–, Comedian, actor, writer
Emma Thompson, 1959–, Comedian, actress, screenwriter
Sandi Toksvig, 1958–, Comedian, writer, radio presenter
Mark Watson, 1980–, Comedian, novelist
Robert Webb, 1972–, Comedian, actor, writer

HUGH'S CAREER
SO FAR

1981, *The Cellar Tapes*, various characters; writer
1983, *Alfresco*, various characters, writer
  The Crystal Cube, Max Belhaven/various characters,
1984, *The Young Ones*, Lord Monty, Episode: 'Bambi'
1985, *Plenty*, Michael
  Mrs Capper's Birthday, Bobby
  Happy Families, Jim
1986, *Blackadder II*, Simon Partridge (also known
  as 'Mr Ostrich' and 'Farters Parters'); Prince Ludwig
  the Indestructible
1987, *Filthy Rich & Catflap*, N'Bend
  Blackadder the Third, George, Prince of Wales,
  Prince Regent
1988, *Blackadder's Christmas Carol*, Prince George
  and Lord Pigmot (future)

1989–1995, *A Bit of Fry and Laurie*, various characters;
also writer

1989, *Blackadder Goes Forth*, Lt the Honourable
George Colhurst St Barleigh
Strapless, Colin
The New Statesman, Waiter

1990–1993, *Jeeves and Wooster*, Bertie Wooster

1992, *Peter's Friends*, Roger Charleston

1993, *All or Nothing at All*, Leo Hopkins

1993–1995, *The Legends of Treasure Island*,
Squire Trelawney (Voice)

1995, *Sense and Sensibility*, Mr Palmer

1996, *Tracey Takes On...*, Timothy Bugge (Season 1)
101 Dalmatians, Jasper

1997, *Spiceworld*, Poirot
The Borrowers, Police Officer Steady
The Ugly Duckling, Tarquin (voice)

1998, *Friends*, Gentleman on the Plane, Episode:
'The One with Ross's Wedding'
The Bill, Harrap
The Man in the Iron Mask, Pierre, The King's Advisor
Cousin Bette, Baron Hector Hulot

1999, *Blackadder: Back & Forth*, Viscount George
Bufton-Tufton/Georgius
Stuart Little, Mr Fredrick Little

2000, *Maybe Baby*, Sam Bell

2001, *Chica de Río* (aka *Girl from Rio*), Raymond Woods
Life with Judy Garland: Me and My Shadows,
Vincente Minnelli
Discovering the Real World of Harry Potter,

Narrator (Voice)

2002, *Stuart Little 2*, Mr Frederick Little

Spooks, Jools Siviter

2003, *The Young Visiters*, Lord Bernard Clark

Fortysomething, Paul Slippery

Stuart Little: The Animated Series, Mr Frederick
Little (Voice), 'The Meatloaf Bandit'

2004–present, *House MD*, Dr Gregory House

2004, *Fire Engine Fred*

Flight of the Phoenix, Ian

2005, *Valiant*, Wing Commander Gutsy (Voice)

The Big Empty, Doctor #5

Stuart Little 3: Call of the Wild, Mr Frederick
Little (Voice)

2006, *Saturday Night Live*, Host, various characters
(Season 32, Episode 4)

2008, *Saturday Night Live*, Host, various characters
(Season 34, Episode 11)

Street Kings, Captain Biggs

2009, *Monsters vs. Aliens*, Dr Cockroach, Ph.D (Voice)

AWARDS FOR *HOUSE*

All of the following are nominations or wins for Laurie's
role as House:

Emmy Awards

2005 – Nominated – Outstanding Lead Actor in a
Drama Series

2007 – Nominated – Outstanding Lead Actor in a
Drama Series

2008 – Nominated – Outstanding Lead Actor in a
Drama Series
2009 – Nominated – Outstanding Lead Actor in a
Drama Series

Golden Globe Awards

2005 – Winner – Best Performance by an Actor
in a Television Series – Drama
2006 – Winner – Best Performance by an Actor
in a Television Series – Drama
2007 – Nominated – Best Performance by an Actor
in a Television Series – Drama
2008 – Nominated – Best Performance by an Actor
in a Television Series – Drama
2009 – Nominated – Best Performance by an Actor
in a Television Series – Drama

Satellite Awards

2005 – Winner – Outstanding Actor in a Series, Drama
2006 – Winner – Outstanding Actor in a Series, Drama
2007 – Nominated – Outstanding Actor in a Series, Drama

Screen Actors Guild Awards

2006 – Nominated – Outstanding Performance
by a Male Actor in a Drama Series
2007 – Winner – Outstanding Performance
by a Male Actor in a Drama Series
2008 – Nominated – Outstanding Performance
by a Male Actor in a Drama Series

2009 – Winner – Outstanding Performance
  by a Male Actor in a Drama Series
2010 – Nominated – Outstanding Performance
  by a Male Actor in a Drama Series

Television Critics Association
2005 – Winner – Individual Achievement in Drama
2006 – Winner – Individual Achievement in Drama
2007 – Nominated – Individual Achievement in Drama

Teen Choice Awards
2006 – Nominated – TV Actor: Drama
2007 – Winner – TV Actor: Drama

People's Choice Awards
2008 – Winner – Favourite Male TV Star
2009 – Nominated – Favourite Male TV Star
  (Results Pending)
2010 – Winner – Favourite Male Drama Actor